Published by Thorston Books

Swaggy Tales

Book Three, Jungle Journey
The Adventures of a Vagabond

© 2014 Jack Stuckmayer
All rights reserved

ISBN 978–0–9887263–5–2

Editor: Harvey Hagman
Book cover and design: Robert Buckner

The dates and names, for the most part, are real. Only a few have been changed to protect the innocent, the guilty or our Swaggy himself.

www.ThorstonBooks.com

Swaggy Tales
Book Three
Jungle Journey
The Adventures of a Vagabond

By Jack Stuckmayer

More true stories from the life of
a transient gentleman.

~~~
# Preface
~~~

From the 1957 Hobos convention in Britt, Iowa:
Hobos will work
Tramps won't work
Bums can't work

I would add to that:
Swaggys must work

A Swaggy does not just travel through the world, but lives in and becomes an integral part of it.

A Swaggy has all his worldly possessions with him, discarding what he cannot carry at each move, and is always home, unlike the hobo, who is never home.

A Swaggy may accept aid from friends and individuals but not from governments or organizations: no welfare, no unemployment compensation and no charity handouts. Friends and individuals can be repaid. Governments and organizations cannot.

A Swaggy must maintain his liberty and live independently.

~ ~~ ~

Dedication

~ ~~ ~

To the kind, helpful, friendly people of Ecuador to whom
we are eternally grateful for helping us through difficult
circumstances, and for sharing their meager substances
with a generosity we had no way to repay.
Thank you.

~~~
# Contents
~~~

Part One
Through Central America by Vehicle

Part Two
Over the Andes in Ecuador by Mule

Part Three
Through the Jungle to the Amazon by Dugout Canoe

~~~
# Prologue
~~~

This book is a narrative of driving through
seven revolutions in Central America,
riding mules across the Andes in Ecuador
and going down the Napo River to the
Amazon in a dugout canoe.

By Jack Stuckmayer

Swaggy Tales
Book Three
The Adventures of a Vagabond
Jungle Journey
by Jack Stuckmayer

~~~

Part One
Through Central America by Vehicle

~~~

~ Plan ~

~~~

Date: February 14 1959
Place: Suburb of Minneapolis, Minnesota
My Age: 24

"This is the sort of damn dumb thing you would do," my brother said as he threw the newspaper at me. "This idiot is going to the jungle to get himself killed." I tried to be nonchalant, but this caught my attention, as he knew it would. I eagerly glomped onto George Grimm's column in the Minneapolis Tribune about a university student who was planning a trip through the jungle and looking for a few kindred spirits to join him. Grimm listed the Minneapolis phone number to call. "This looks interesting," I mumbled to myself.

"Interesting? Interesting?" my brother shouted. "He's going to drive through revolutions in Central America, fly to Ecuador, cross the Andes by mule and take a dugout canoe through the Amazon jungle. That's not interesting, that's insane!" He stomped off in disgust. I read the story carefully and five minutes later was on the phone calling Jay, the student planning the trip.

Phone calls to Minneapolis were long distance. This call could cost me several dollars, which I didn't have, but I was enticed. This could be my escape from having to get a steady job as a teacher or working for some corporation. I had already squandered my first year and a half out of college, seeking fortune in California and Oregon and failing miserably. Now the pressure was on from friends and family to settle down. I was doomed to live a normal life unless, unless. . .

The operator connected the call – it wasn't fast, easy or cheap in those days – and a voice said "Hello."

"Hello," I replied, "is Jay available?"

"I'm Jay,"

"Ah. My name is Jack and I just read George Grimm's column in the Tribune about the trip you're planning."

"Yes. We plan to leave in early June, but there is a lot of preparation to be done first." He had a reassuring voice, confident and stable. I already liked him.

"Well, it sounds like fun and I'd like to join you." Fun was the wrong word and I was too eager to commit myself but was afraid that he would have so many wanting to go that there might not be room for me.

"Fun! Fun!" my brother shouted from the next room. "Who's paying for this call?" I covered the mouthpiece and shouted back, "I'll pay for it, don't worry."

"Fun, fun," he went on. "Some fun."

"You're running up my phone bill, why don't you just read the rest of the paper?" I shouted back, and uncovered the mouthpiece.

"I live thirty miles out of Minneapolis," I said to Jay, "and would like to talk to you about it, if you have room for one more."

"We're meeting Wednesday evening at seven," he said "at Coffman Memorial Union at the University of Minnesota." We, he said, we. How many were there already? Was there room for one more?

"I'll be there." And that was it. This telephone call changed the direction of my life but I didn't know that at the time. I was just trying to temporarily escape a dull, dreary existence.

My life up to this point is pretty well covered in several chapters in Swaggy Tales, Books One and Two. My two brothers, six and nine years older than me, had both quit high school at age 16 to join the Navy during World War. They each married at age 19 and now each has a wife and four children to support. They made their decisions at a young age. Families are wonderful but I did not want to follow their example and commit myself to a normal life. However, as stated previously, the pressure was on. I thought, if I could just get on the jungle trip I could put the life decision off for another eight or nine months and who knows what might or might not happen. We could get shot by rebels in Central America, which would solve all my problems, or find a fortune in gold in the deep, dark jungle as depicted monthly in True and Argosy magazines – or maybe be rescued by a beautiful tribal princess. My mind was already dancing in the world of fantasy, but I quickly returned to earth remembering that an experienced adventurer had said there are no beautiful tribal princesses. "When the native women start looking good it's time to get the hell out of the jungle." His description of life in the jungle was not romantic.

My life was at low ebb after my recent ear operation, a tympanoplasty, had failed. I was stuck with chronic Otitis Media, a middle ear infection that drained through my perforated ear drum. The alternative was to seal off the drum and leave me deaf in my right ear; but no. I would rather have some hearing in each ear so when I sing in a chorus I can hear both sides. I could live with the condition and thought "Medicine is advancing, maybe someday…"

The 1950s were a time of prosperity. Jobs were plentiful and spirits were high, but people who had struggled through the Depression surrounded me. "Get a job and stick with it" was standard advice. It didn't matter what kind of job as long as you were working. And "If you don't get married and settle down you'll never have anything." Steady work and marriage solved all life's problems. There were few single men over the age of twenty two in my village. Both brothers made a gloomy prognosis for me, "You're going to end up like Roy." Roy was in his forties, retarded, and made a dollar a day hoisting milk cans for Clayton, the dairy truck driver.

"You judge everything by money," I said. "I want to experience life, not just work at the same job for 40 years. I want to have fun, excitement, adventure."

They smiled. "You want to be a playboy." I let this pass, not knowing what a playboy was. "Well, Roy will have to retire someday. We'll ask Clayton to give you a chance when the time comes."

Wednesday came and I found Coffman Memorial Union. Jay was tall; nice looking with dark hair, had a pleasant disposition and a sonorous voice. I introduced myself. He said Harvey and Lenny couldn't come tonight and got right into the details of the trip.

"You'll need a passport, which will take a few weeks to get. Then you must apply for visas to seven Central American countries and four in South America. I'll help with that. They don't always respond quickly, sometimes not at all. You have to keep at them; be persistent. They're having a lot of revolutions."

"Thanks," I said. "Glad for your help. Which ones are having revolutions?" I asked apprehensively.

"Nobody seems to know," Jay answered. "The class in Latin American studies here at the U doesn't have much to go on. They know Nicaragua is controlled by the army and think there may be five or six other revolutions in progress now, but they really don't know. They give us less than a fifty percent chance of returning alive if we go as planned." I gave him a puzzled look.

He continued, "I think they're wrong. We're just students passing through. No threat to anyone. Everyone likes students. They won't bother us." A real optimist, I thought. "Also," he went on, changing the subject, "You'll need seventeen shots and vaccinations against exotic jungle diseases to be given over a period of weeks."

He had researched everything thoroughly and gave me a list of the things to be done. I immediately liked Jay and was looking forward to spending time with him. Then, casually, "We each need to have $600 travel money."

This hit me like a ton of bricks, I hadn't thought of money. How could I save that much in just three months? I was making $50 a week at the locker plant and could probably save $25 of that. My mind was already pondering how to make more money and save it. But that could wait; I'll work it out somehow. We talked about a reason for the trip that I could use to explain it to my family and friends. Just for fun and adventure was not enough. This trip, in their eyes, was a frivolous waste of time and money. I needed an excuse. Jay had one.

"We will look for and assay minerals in the rivers. I will test the rivers with dithiozone for cobalt, nickel and copper. Then we will find a way to trace and mine it. This trip could make us a fortune." Jay smiled. He knew this was baloney, but it would work. We were seeking fortune, not adventure.

The book, Rivers Ran East, by Leonard Clark, had inspired Jay to make the trip. He told me a little about it. We talked for a while and exchanged addresses. I left with a lot of questions unanswered but felt everything would work out; Jay was a natural leader. As it turned out I soon quit the locker plant and went back to making Popsicles at Jersey Ice Cream Co. in Minneapolis which paid $2.58 per hour (with overtime this came to $120 per week), enough to cover the trip. Also my next older brother worked at the creamery with my father and had a barn painting business on the side. I helped him on weekends. Our older brother owned a filling station and also could use part-time help.

I applied for a passport and made arrangements with our

young family doctor, who was a friend, to get the required shots. Things were moving along. One problem arose. Some countries wanted a bank statement with the application for a visa. I had no bank account. My local bank did not want to go through the trouble of starting an account for me, knowing I would withdraw the funds and leave in a couple months. My brother interceded, making sure the banker knew he thought the jungle trip was a stupid idea.

I read Rivers Ran East, by Leonard Clark, but was not convinced. It was too much like articles in True and Argosy magazines, snakes hanging out of every tree, savages blowing poison darts and head hunters who could shrink your head to two and a half inches. I went to the library and read about Orellana, the Spanish explorer who in the 1540's, starting from Quito, Ecuador, crossed the Andes and went down the Napo River to the Amazon, getting attacked by a tribe of female savages in the process. He then went the full length of the Amazon searching for gold. During his trip, hundreds of his men were killed (many by poisoned darts) or died from jungle causes. He himself died of illness and grief. This was the route we planned to follow.

I received a postcard saying our next meeting was Friday, March 27th, at the same place. Good. I was eager to meet the rest of the crew.

Jay was there with Harvey, tall, skinny, fair haired and younger than the rest of us, only 19. The best way to describe Harvey is exuberant youth – smiling, joking, laughing, telling stories. Good company. They were revamping Harvey's 1950 Chevrolet sedan, which had twice been reclaimed from death by junking; first by a garbage collector who cut it up into a pickup then junked it again to be reclaimed by Harvey. Harvey was also an optimist. He and Jay were building a wooden structure just behind the front seat, to accommodate two riders in discarded theater seats, leaving room for our baggage. I didn't see this creative concoction until the day we left or I might have rethought the whole thing. But I was ready for adventure.

Jay had run an ad in the University student paper about the trip. Harvey, who was planning to be a journalist, saw the ad, liked the idea and decided to go along as far as Costa Rica, then continue on to visit a pen pal in Chile. He feared snakes and the jungle. He took the story to George Grimm in hopes of gaining more recruits. Several had expressed interest, but didn't sign up.

"Is that all?" I asked. "Are we it?" I couldn't believe that we were the only ones interested in this great adventure. Half the men at the U should be signing up.

"No, Lenny is coming," Jay said. "He's a junior in psychology, has his passport and is applying for visas." He calls once in a while to ask how things are going. And there may be one more, Jake. Maybe. Only saw him once, but he says he's going."

Lenny, being a junior in psychology, bothered me. He reminded me of my friend, Anton who was schizoid (Swaggy Tales, Book One). Some time later a young man swaggered in. "Sorry I'm late. Got tied up with a business deal." Jay introduced him as Jake who was thinking of joining us.

"Thinking of joining you? I'm going and that's it," he said. "You can count on me. I've had a lot of experience and have read enough to know how to get through revolutions. You have to be firm and self-confident. And the jungle won't be a problem for me. I'm used to living in tough conditions." He went on and on. He was working his way through college as a salesman, selling hope chest items to single women. I didn't trust him.

Jay waited patiently and then explained that maybe none of us would be able to go. Nicaragua's revolution was exploding in turmoil.

"Well I'm going," Jake said. "I don't care if the rest of you chicken out. I'll go by myself," he said, waving his arms. "No little revolution is going to hold me back." Then, looking at his watch, he said, "I have to go. See you at the next meeting."

"Try to make it on time," Harvey said with a smile. When he was gone, Harvey continued, "It wouldn't bother me to dump him off in the middle of a Nicaraguan revolution."

"I don't think he'll be joining us," Jay said. "He doesn't have his passport yet."

We hoped the Nicaragua revolution would soon be over and we kept planning. Jungle hammocks, sleeping bags, duffle bags, white gas camp stove, dutch oven, pots, and other items we could get at an army surplus store. We would each buy our own sleeping bag and jungle hammock. I said I would bring canned goods. We decided to meet again in six weeks and parted friends. I liked them both and felt comfortable about the trip. No more was said about Lenny, who hadn't shown up.

Second Meeting - April, 1959, Minnesota

I found another book, Andes and the Amazon, by James Orton, who had followed the route taken by Orellana, the conquistador, in 1867, the same route we planned to take. Orton described the trails and villages in detail. It would all be different now, 90 years later. In the 16th century it is believed there were five million natives living in the Amazon basin. Few are left. Most died of diseases brought by the European invaders. I was sorry to read that the female Amazon warriors were also gone; there's something romantic about being attacked by bare breasted, spear carrying, shrieking female savages. Not a bad way to go. Harvey could write an obituary for us in the Minnesota Daily.

Orton wrote, "A footpath, open only in the dry season, and barely passable then, connects Quito and the Rio Napo." This was our planned trail but that was nearly a hundred years ago. I was sure by now there is a well maintained road. We should have no trouble. Orton described the Quechua Indians as peaceful and tranquil, living in poverty amid potential wealth.

Our next meeting was Friday, May 22nd. I meant to ask Jay how he picked his route and if he knew we were following the route of Orellana, but never did, too many other things to talk about.

Once again at Coffman Memorial Union it was just Harvey, Jay and I. I asked about Lenny.

"He'll be here," Jay said. Lenny was from a town north of the Twin Cities. His father had been successful in the insurance business so he had never had to work and didn't bat an eye about the $600. That's all Jay knew.

Everything was shaping up. The car/truck was nearly ready; we each had our own hammocks and sleeping bags. I got my covered hammock from an army surplus store and had to restring it after the rotten strings broke and dumped me onto the basement floor. So much for old army surplus. We had a gas camping stove, canteens, cast iron frying pan, pots, kettles, a gas lantern and miscellaneous items we each thought might be needed. Fact is we had no idea what we needed. I had a large duffle bag filled with canned goods. Some visas had not come but there was still time. We decided to meet on the 13th at my parent's house in the suburbs and leave from there. My mother wanted to prepare a good breakfast for us so we could begin our journey on a full belly.

Finally Lenny arrived. Jay introduced us and filled Lenny in on recent decisions. He didn't seem concerned. He'd go along with any reasonable propositions. He was aloof, smiling condescendingly at we lesser beings. His stance, mannerisms and way of speech were so similar to Anton that I thought he might also be a functioning schizophrenic. He was self-centered. I hoped my life never depended on him. But here he was, part of the crew. So be it. I smiled graciously, determined to make the best of it.

I said nothing to Jay and Harvey about my apprehensions. Jay was stable and could put up with anyone and Harvey wouldn't be bothered. I imagined Lenny would classify us as neurotics. Other psychology students I knew all had problems that they hoped to overcome by studying Freud. To compensate they rationalized, pointing out the neurosis of classmates.

We finalized plans and exchanged parent's names, addresses and telephone numbers. Next time we met would be on the day we left, June 13th. We didn't know each other well. I had only met Harvey twice and Lenny once. But we were all young, healthy Minnesotans who had grown up with the Christian ethic, with enough in common to let us learn from each other, maybe enough to carry us through difficult times ahead. Jay gave us each a copy of the itinerary, subject to change.

Proposed Itinerary

Date	Place	Transportation
June 13, 1959	Leave Minneapolis	Harvey's van
June 14, 1959	Arrive Houston, Texas	Harvey's van
June 17, 1959	Mexico City	Harvey's van
June 28, 1959	San Jose, Costa Rica	Harvey's van
July 4, 1959	Quito, Ecuador	By Air
July 5, 1959	Tena, Ecuador	By Mule
August 1, 1959	Iquitos, Peru	By dugout canoe
August 8, 1959	Manaos, Brazil	Canoe or Riverboat
August 20, 1959	Belem, Brazil	Canoe or Riverboat
August 31, 1959	San Jose, Costa Rica	By Air
September 15, 1959	Minneapolis	By Air

It was well thought out and could be revised if necessary. Jay had also mapped out a mileage chart for the trip through Central America:

Minneapolis, Minnesota to Humble, Texas	1,176
Houston – Brownsville, Texas	389
Brownsville – Mexico City	41

To Zanatapec, Mexico	528
To Tapachula, (by rail) Mexico	261
To Guatemala City, Guatemala	207
To Managua, Nicaragua	640
To Cartago, Costa Rica	375
Total miles	4,217

As it turned out, the three of us had to meet again in early June. Harvey managed to get the Minneapolis Star to do a story on our trip and a spot on the local TV news. The Star took our pictures and did an article on us to appear the day we left. Another adventurer, also in the news, named Harold, was going down the Mississippi in a canoe. The TV interviewer asked us if we thought we would reach the Gulf before him. "I'm putting my money on Harold," Harvey retorted. Harvey was going to make a good journalist and a good travel companion.

Vehicle Concerns - Saturday, June 13th, 1959, Minnesota

Finally the much planned day of departure arrived. The three of them drove into my parent's driveway, just off Highway 12 west of Minneapolis. I got my first serious look at our mode of transportation. The body of the twice-junked 1950 Chevy was cut off just behind the driver's door with a 6 foot by 8 foot box like structure built behind it out of rough cut lumber. Harvey referred to this as the "living area." The driver's door was welded shut because it would not stay closed and the exhaust pipe ended just before the "living area" which meant the fumes flowed freely to engulf the two passengers sitting on seats rescued from the now defunct Radio City Theater in downtown Minneapolis. The two polygonal open-air windows promised to help a bit. I wondered what chance the class in Latin American studies at the U of M would give us now if they saw our vehicle.

"We revamped the motor, installed new brake shoes and put in overload springs," Harvey said proudly. I don't know whom the we meant (neither he nor Jay were mechanically minded) but Harvey had many friends. For my part I had already owned a half-dozen old cars which could be purchased for $25 to $35 and had learned how to keep them running. I was designated the mechanic and brought my box of basic hand tools.

My mother looked on kindly, but skeptically, at the red painted wooden box on the van with MPLS. – COSTA RICO CON SUERTE (Minneapolis to Costa Rico with luck) painted in large white letters on the side. She just smiled, said quietly, "God will look after you all," and invited us in for a working man's breakfast of scrambled eggs, fried potatoes, bacon, ham, pancakes, toast, butter, milk and coffee. She had also packed us a lunch. Ah, what a world that was to live in, when full-time mothers were in charge. That breakfast was one of the meals Jay, Lenny and I would remember and discuss weeks later when we ran out of food in the middle of the Amazon jungle. But for now we had stuffed bellies and hearts full of hope anticipating great adventure.

After a leisurely breakfast we discussed supplies. Visas had been a problem along with all the necessary shots, bank statements, police records, etc., that were sent back and forth several times. Latin American bureaucrats are skilled in obfuscation. Harvey's visa from Honduras had still not arrived. It would hopefully catch up with us in Texas. We had bulk water cans, gas cans, oil cans, two duffle bags of canned food, hammocks and personal items. Harvey, at the last minute, came up with a case of Spam and a case of baked beans, which turned out to be of great benefit, except for the last can which nearly proved to be fatal, but more of that later. I have not eaten Spam since.

Atop our "living quarters" were most of our 13 spare tires, some on rims, strapped to an upside down bedspring. Size six by sixteen used tires from junked cars were cheap and plentiful.

A quick look told me most didn't have a hundred miles left on them. Jay, Lenny and I each had rifles and I had borrowed a 22 caliber pistol from my brother. Why, I don't know, I had no intention of shooting anyone, especially in Latin America where you could get interred for life for an automobile accident. Many such stories had already reached us.

The Minneapolis Star printed the picture of us. I quote from Harvey's notation, written later: "The fellow with the long, black hair is our leader, Jay, our spark-plug. He's in his fourth year of chemistry at the U of Minnesota. Jack, up top, has not yet grown his dust-blonde beard, as it is taboo in the Popsicle factory where he's employed. Jack, with a bachelor's degree in music, is in charge of saying philosophical nothings to stimulate or begin aimless discussions. I'm the skinny blonde, 19, with a nearly invisible goatee. I am a journalism major who has not worked at the college paper nor yet had a course in journalism. My grandmother told us 'Now you boys be careful. Harvey, be sure to say hello to your Aunt Effie in Seattle. I wrote and told her you were coming.' I never could explain that we were not going through Seattle. She was deaf. Aunt Effie is still waiting. Grams cried. 'Be careful and take all your vitamin pills,' Jack's mother tells him. 'Today's blue, tomorrow yellow and don't forget to rotate your colors.'"

My butter maker father could not get away from the creamery. Cans of milk need to be dumped, weighed and tested seven days a week. I hugged my mother, speculating it might be the last time, and we were off.

Well, not quite "off." I had requested to be the first driver and slid into the driver's seat through the passenger's door. Harvey slid in next to me, while Jay and Lenny occupied the "living quarters" in the back.

"Harvey," I said, stepping on the starter and getting no reaction, "It's not turning over."

"Oh, yeah," he answered. "It does that sometimes and we

have to push. But it runs fine once it gets going." He, Jay and Lenny jumped out, pushed the car back down the driveway, then forward up the street. I dropped it in high gear and popped the clutch. It started. We were now officially "off." We either had a bad battery or a malfunctioning generator. I said nothing. I didn't want to turn back now that we had started but it would have to be dealt with somewhere down the road. "*Mio problema*" I said to myself, already starting to think in Spanish.

I remember noting the time, 1:15. I don't know why I thought that was important but I still remember it now, more than 50 years later. It was good to be on our way but once on the road I couldn't help but notice a howl in the differential before were even on the main highway. "Harvey," I said, "Your differential is howling."

"Oh, yeah, it always does that. Been doing that since I first got the vehicle. It's nothing. Just ignore it." I realized that being the designated mechanic was going to have its drawbacks. None of them would understand our vehicle had one bearing in the grave, so to speak. Too late now, we were underway, so I suggested we sing.

Someone knew the words to what became our theme song, *Cuanta La Gusta*. We all learned it and sang it again and again. It is scarcely remembered now, 50 years later, that in those days, everyone sang. Even those who were alive at that time don't remember. We all knew songs from the Golden Book, hymn books, sheet music and songs handed down by our grandparents. We sang, maybe around a fire in the woods with guitars or around the piano in someone's living room, or walking down the street. All this changed when television became the national addiction. No more singing, no more participation in life. Americans became spectators, sitting in front of the television set watching nonsense and buying the products advertised. Sad. But I digress.

We sang, "*Cuanta la gus ta la gusta la gus ta la gus ta la gus ta la gus ta la gusta. Cuanta la gusta la gus ta la gus ta la gus ta la gus ta la gusta.* We gotta get goin, where we goin, what're we gonna do? We're on our way to somewhere, the three of us and you." At this place we each pointed at someone else. "Who will be there, what'll we see there, what'll be the big surprise? There may be *señoritas* with dark and flashing eyes. We're on our way, pack up your pack. And if we stay, we won't come back. How can we go? We haven't got a dime, but we're goin and we're gonna have a happy time." A singable song that suited us perfectly.

We made it all the way to Spring Valley, Minnesota by 5:15 pm, just over a hundred miles, before our first breakdown. The generator gave out. We picked one up at a local junkyard, I installed it and we pressed on, undeterred. Well, I was deterred, but what did I know? I was just the mechanic. Again we sang *Cuanta La Gusta.*

We switched off driving and drove all night; the exhaust fumes in the "living quarters" irritating the sleepers in the back. Had our first flat tire at 10 am the next morning. The voltage regulator became a chronic problem that had to be ignored. Outside of that the van was running fairly well. We picked up more groceries from Harvey's friends in Davenport, Iowa, and drove all night the second night. Lenny started running a fever, he said, and had to sit in the front seat, away from the exhaust fumes. That left only the three of us to drive. Twice we pulled over and slept for a while.

Minnesota to Texas

Getting started

~~~

~ Part One: Travel ~

~~~

Sunday, June 14th, On the road

Operation Meatballs: Our sandwiches were gone. I warmed canned meatballs on the Coleman stove held by Harvey, precariously balanced on a cross beam between the two open-air windows. This was before the freeway system and the overload springs kept the van continuously bouncing. As I attempted to pass Jay an aluminum foil plate through the cab window, it tipped and dumped gravy on our maps. After that we pulled over to cook.

Monday, June 15th, Humble, Texas

We arrived at Jay's uncle Justice's home, in Humble, Texas,

Ready or not - the highways and byways beckon

*Does anyone want to guess
how many miles are left on these well used tires?*

just north of Houston. We were welcomed with true southern hospitality. It was nice to sit in a chair that didn't continually bounce. Justice's nephew, Kent, was visiting while his parents were on vacation. Kent said, "Let's take them froggin'. I want to go froggin'." Sounded fine to us, so we picked up the frog spears and walked out to the pond. Texas frogs are huge. We came back with a half dozen, enough for breakfast.

After a nice meal Jay answered questions about our planned trip. He laid out the agenda: "We will drive down the Pan-American Highway, fly to Quito, Ecuador, cross the Andes by mule, go down the Napo River by dugout canoe to the Amazon River. Then we go on to Iquitos, Peru, a city surrounded by jungle. From there we will travel another thousand miles by canoe or mail boat to Manaos, Brazil, ending up in Belem, another thousand miles further, on the Atlantic coast." I listened intently, not having really thought seriously about the details before. Seems like a lot of canoeing through the jungle. I had a vague idea of what a dugout canoe was, a hollowed out tree trunk, but had never seen one. The canoes used on Minnesota lakes moved right along with good paddlers, a dugout must be slower. But would I want to paddle a thousand miles? Seemed a long way. Well, I'm sure Jay has it all worked out. Jay went on to explain that with our guns and basic necessities we would live off jungle abundance, just like the natives.

Lenny interjected "We only have enough medicine for one man, not three." This passed without comment. I wondered what medicine he was talking about? I didn't know we had anything more than a first aid kit and vitamin pills. And what brought up the subject?

Harvey talked about his trip to Cuba the year before; he, the youngest, was the only one of us to have been off the North American continent. "I'm only along to Costa Rica, not to the jungle. I don't like snakes. Then I'll fly to Chili to visit a pen pal."

We were getting to know each other. Harvey and his younger sister were adopted from the Swedish Institute. Their adoptive mother died when he was 13, his adoptive father left right after the funeral, leaving he and his sister to live with their grandmother on Grams' social security payments of $28 per month. His father kept the monthly Social Security payments of $180 for each of them and stayed drunk the rest of his life. But Grams and the kids stuck together and made the best of it. They were close. Harvey had a tough life but was equal to it, always laughing and joking. Jay had grown up in a normal home. His father was raised in an orphanage. He and Jay's mother had adopted a boy just older than Jay.

I never did learn any details about Lenny except that he had an older sister and his father was financially successful. To entertain our hosts Lennie played Jazz on the piano and I played some light classics. I couldn't help noticing Lenny's hands; they had never done physical work.

The fact is this was to be a hurried trip through Central America, not a sight seeing expedition. We were inexperienced young travelers just trying to get through the revolutions without getting shot. We didn't know how to avoid getting sick from the food and water but would take our chances. The jungle was our destination and everything revolved around that.

Tuesday, June 16th, Humble, Texas

After a good night's sleep in a real bed, we had frog for breakfast. I had frog legs before but never the whole frog. Interesting, tasty. Harvey's visa hadn't come back from the Honduras Consulate in New York so we had to lay over another night.

While we gassed up a friend of Justices pulled in. He had oil (pronounced all) wells that pumped $250 a day. Oil sells for $3 per barrel. His oil comes from a salt dome under his land.

"You going to foot the bill, Mista Sheffield?" Justice asks.

"Sure, why not? Got to show these Yanks some southern hospitality."

So Jay got two extra quarts of oil, had a tire mounted and filled the gas tank. Can't beat southern hospitality.

Justice drove us to a rodeo stadium. We checked out the corral. Lenny had read somewhere about a way to stop a charging bull and said, "If a bull charged me, I'd punch him in the nose."

Justice smiled. "And he'd break your arm."

"Oh." End of conversation on rodeos.

Justice took us along while he checked some of his oil wells. It was very hot and this was the first time any of us had been in an air conditioned car. Back at the house Harvey and I got on Justice's horse. It bucked. Harvey fell off and didn't get back on.

That evening more of Jay's relatives came over, more oil people. Lenny had the chance to be the center of attention and entertained them by hypnotizing Kent. He fooled Kent into thinking the first people he saw were his parents. Kent was so happy to see them. Everyone was impressed. I thought it cruel. Kent was brought back with no memory of the event.

Wednesday, June 17th, Humble, Texas

Harvey's visa arrived. Nicaragua is being invaded again. "We may have to lose our beards," someone said.

"We may lose our heads," someone retorted as we drove to the Mexican Consulate in Houston to get our visas.

"Do you think that thing can make it to Guatemala?" the counsel asked, looking at our banged up truck. "Those roads are pretty bad."

"Well, our van is pretty bad too, so we should make it," Jay answered.

Harvey and I had our pictures taken in a rundown studio. With my few days growth of beard I looked like an escaped convict. Harvey went from blond to a dark complexion on the photo.

We got our Mexican visas. They didn't care about our guns.

That evening after a dinner of southern fried chicken (one of the wonderful meals we would remember in the jungle) I sat down at the piano and asked if anyone wanted to sing hymns.

"I went to Bible camp and all we did was sing those blasted hymns," said Jay.

"Just follow the lower notes," I said.

"All notes are just a bunch of fly crap to me," Jay said.

We sang hymns around the piano. Someone said, "First one to stop pays two dollars." No one wants to be the first but we finally quit singing to enjoy the peaceful Texas evening. Anticipating difficult times I recorded my weight, 169. Harvey took inventory for the coming border crossing. Everything was ready. We were carefree young men about to start on an adventure and eager to get on with it. We were two days behind schedule already. We thanked Justice and his family for their kindness, said goodbye and left just before eight p.m. for the Mexican border at Brownsville, Texas, 400 miles south, singing Quan Tela Gusta, over and over.

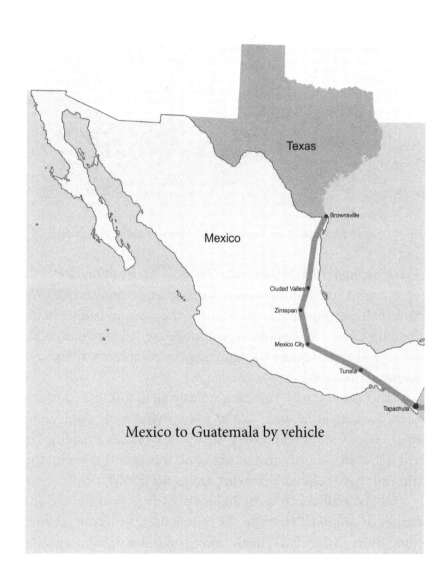

Mexico to Guatemala by vehicle

The author (designated mechanic) pondering the viability of the vehicle.

Thursday, June 18th, Brownsville, Texas — Mexican Border

It took three hours to cross the border at Brownsville. We hauled all our bags and luggage out of the van and laid them on the long table. The customs agent looked at the duffle of food, the case of Spam, cans of beans, camping equipment, rifles, and threw up his hands.

"This is too much. You cannot bring all of this into Mexico." Then, looking at us said, "*No se puede.*" (It is not possible, no way.) He waved his hands over the whole works as a finality. He had not even opened most of our stuff. It is over, I thought, the trip ends here before we even get across the border.

Jay just smiled and spoke to him politely in Spanish. He understood "*Mordida*" (the bite, the bribe), the only way to get anything done in Mexico. Finally, after some discussion, Jay gave him six dollars. He smiled, shook hands with all of us and wished us a good trip.

Three or four dollars might have been enough, but would

have involved time and haggling. Six dollars was generous and got us through quickly with not a word about our guns. Actually, for six dollars we could have brought in a cannon. Jay was prepared; we were not. He was our leader, but never had to lead. We followed. We piled back into our vehicle, (which I will, from here on, call the van) and pressed on, singing *Cuanta La Gusta*, already dreaming of *señoritas* with dark and flashing eyes.

Jay was our translator. Harvey had been to Cuba and I had one semester of Spanish, Lenny knew little. So Jay got us through the tough spots. We wondered if anyone had driven the full length of the Pan American highway and if so, why? It was safe to assume we were not the first; travel in Central America was common. The Mexican *peso* was worth eight U.S. cents. Cigarettes were selling for 25 cents a pack in the states, Mexican cigarettes sold for fifty *centavos* a pack (half a *peso*), less than four cents. They were good. The young Mexican women were beautiful.

Soon we realized that we had entered a world of poverty. People live in mud huts that would not serve for cattle in the US. Garbage and filth were everywhere. Minnesotans would be cleaning, washing, scrubbing and building. Here they live with it and in it.

Finding a place, thirty feet off the main highway in a stream bed we backed in to cook supper and have a night's sleep. Canned chili and crackers, tea and canned pears. We drew for 2½ hour watches starting at 8 pm. It was very hot and humid. Well into Harvey's watch, , it began to rain hard. Jay asked, "Do we stay or go?" Fearing we may wash away, we vote to leave. Jay asked Harvey to find his poncho. Lenny couldn't find his either. Rain was dripping down my back, our living quarters were not waterproof. I started the van. We were stuck in mud. They pushed with mud flying from the spinning wheels. We managed to reach the highway. Harvey's boots were mud outside, water inside. We were soaked. It rained and rained. I drove until 4 am when it started to clear. We stopped, laid our clothes on the hood and on top the van and on the nearby rocks and tied our boots to the sides to dry. The first night of our adventure was miserable, yet enjoyable. The sun rose bright and warm. After brewing coffee and having a breakfast of Spam and beans (not a typical Minnesota breakfast, but we are roughing it) we started off again in good spirits.

Friday, June 19th, Ciudad Valles, Mexico

The road was narrow and full of potholes but by evening we arrived in Ciudad Valles (341 miles from the border) and rented a hotel room for 80 *pesos* ($6.40). Hardly any bugs. Very nice. Lenny was first to leave for the cantina and was cavorting with the marimba band by the time we got there. Lenny was with us but not really part of the group, in the pancake, so to speak, but not part of the dough. He reminded me more and more of my schizoid friend Anton. I will keep my eye on him and hope he doesn't cause a major problem.

The band had a wonderful guitar player.

Saturday, June 20th, Ciudad Valles, Mexico

Had my first slice of fresh pineapple with breakfast, delicious. Just as we were leaving, a man on the street showed me a nice guitar for only 130 *pesos* ($10.30). What a deal! I snapped it up. Once on our way I tried to play it. *No se puede*! It was a piece of junk. Each fret has to be 1/18th of the remaining length of the string. These were placed at random, completely useless. I gave it to the first Mexican kid I saw, who will probably sell it to some other gringo tourist. I still had my own cheap, but functional, guitar, which I will not part with.

Sunday, June 21st, Zimapan, Mexico

Drove in the mountains all day through fog on curvy roads.

Only made it 177 miles to Zimapan where we got a room with a lovely ceramic patio at the hotel, Fundicion, for 60 *pesos*. This is living. Poverty, burros and Coca Cola signs have been ubiquitous. The bouncing is taking its toll on our entrails. Our pace of life has slowed to that of the natives. We can relax tonight and leave for Mexico City in the morning. The AAA book says you can drive from Texas to Mexico City in 10 hours. It's taking us four days. We are behind Jay's schedule, but not to worry, things will certainly pick up.

Monday, June 22nd, Mexico City

I hated to leave Zimapan, such a peaceful environment with a lovely mountain view from our patio. The last 180 miles to Mexico City passed without incident but once there we had to pay the outrageous sum of 64 *pesos* for a hotel room. Lenny's father supposedly had a guide lined up for us, but we never connected so we found our own guide, or rather he found us, as they do in Mexico and gave us a tour of the city. He took us to two brothels, the most popular stop for young American tourists.

The young girls were beautiful, incredibly beautiful. Prostitution is a way out of abject poverty. Whatever other jobs are available aren't viable. Being a mistress of a successful man is another option, but that's only temporary, or marriage. But marriage often brings a dozen children and permanent poverty. I would like to know how many do make their way to a better life.

So, here we were with beautiful girls sitting on our laps, tousling our hair and smiling enticingly. We all succumbed and signed traveler's checks. Later Jay and I couldn't recall much about the whole event but Lenny and Harvey were rhapsodic. It was the first time Harvey had been with a woman sexually and he wrote a three page dissertation, elaborating every detail.

We still had to get visas for Nicaragua from its consulate in Mexico City. This involved another photo. We were starting to look like criminals in our photos. Evidently the army and police have things under control and the country is open to tourists. Harvey walked to the embassy and found out he didn't need a visa for Chile. There were eight revolutions going on in Central and South America. The American Consulate told us they didn't have any specific warnings and advised us to "play it by ear," whatever that meant, but we weren't about to turn back. It is hard to be frightened about something so nebulous. The Pan American Highway was not finished so Jay and I booked passage on the railroad from Tonala, Mexico to Tapachula on the border with Guatemala, a trip of about a hundred and twenty miles. Our reservations are for Friday June 26th. Hope we make it.

We have eaten quite a bit of questionable food but as yet have not gotten sick, but expect to before the end of trip. Jay may have had a recurrence of his previous sickness, endocarditis, yesterday but seems to feel better today. They drive to beat hell down here, taxis especially. Don't use lights until very dark. Peddlers come to us like flies to manure.

Tuesday, June 23rd, Mexico City

Lenny went out on the town last night while the rest of us prepared for the arduous trip ahead. Money is no problem for him. We didn't ask him what he did and he didn't say. Lenny is worried about getting back home by September 15. The rest of us are worried about getting back home, period.

We loaded up in front of the hotel. A man from Hibbing, Minnesota, happened to be walking past and suggested to Harvey that he paint "estudiantes" on the sides of the van. Latin Americans like students, they are always ready to revolt and cause trouble. A crowd gathered about while he was painting and gave us a warm send off. We had to ask directions while leaving the city and twice drivers stopped and held up traffic to give us directions.

Once out of the city we were back in peasant country. The Indian women of the mountains are not as pretty as those in Mexico City. Had another flat. Drove all night.

Wednesday, June 24th, In the mountains

I made us a breakfast of stew and mashed potatoes. Harvey didn't eat. He had diarrhea and a temperature and sweated a great deal. Said he is sick in mind and body. The mountain roads are very bad, curvy and bumpy, which makes life miserable for him. He sleeps most of the day. We were worried about not having enough food. Late afternoon Harvey awoke and opened a can of soup, which I chewed him out for, unjustly, and said, "Okay, tomorrow you take over as cook." I later relented, apologized and stayed on as cook.

We spent the night camped by the side of the road. Bugs were terrible while the light lantern was on. Lenny slung his hammock in the trees, Jay slept on the ground next to the car. Harvey and I slept in the car.

Thursday, June 25th, Tonala, Mexico

Got an early start and arrived in Tonala soon enough to get on the train today, a day before scheduled. While waiting to get on the train, several boys came up and asked if we wanted *hielo*, which we finally realized meant ice. Young boys begging were common and we often gave them a few *pesos*, not yet realizing that this would encourage them to keep begging, sometimes into adulthood. When they came back with the ice we paid them nine *pesos*, the agreed on price. This caused a great argument, as there were eight boys.

There were three cars on our flatcar and one on the other. First, a professor and family with an exchange student, Roberto, from Guatemala City. Next, us. Then two fellows from North Carolina, Nate and Alec in a new Ford, with which they just had an accident. Nate was tall lean and dark. Alec is light, blond and a little heavier. They plan to drive all the way to Brazil and sell their car. Might turn out to be quite an adventure, we've heard stories about how rough and dangerous Brazil is. The flatcar behind us has two couples from Texas, drinking heavily, and bitching about the stupid Mexicans. Fortunately we have little contact with them, being on different flatcars.

We can see Mexico's backside from the train, as we pass swamps, mountains and out-of-the-way villages. It is hot but fun just to take in all the scenery from the train. Harvey says his body is shrinking and getting darker. One of my prize possessions was a ten gallon hat I bought in Oregon on the chrome mining fiasco. I tightened the chin strap while standing on the flatcar and stuck my head in the car window to tell Jay and Lenny to be careful with their hats, as it was very windy. When I pulled my head out my hat blew off and disappeared. Some Mexican peasant was the recipient of a $10 hat which might be too big for him but sale-able. Just as well. It's not good to have something valuable to worry about and protect on a trip like this.

As it started to darken we got out the stove, kettle, two cans of beef stew, one can of potatoes and three cans of corn, planning to cook a stew for the nine of us. Suddenly the train stopped with a lurch in a village. People gathered around the flatcar, some carrying tin plates and cups. It is a custom to feed everyone. We didn't have enough food so I just stopped cooking. Some music flowed from a distant source. Nate got out his trumpet and I played guitar. We sang *Cielito Lindo* with them and became the center of a fiesta. It was romantic Mexico in action. Spontaneity.

Small boys ran across our flatcar and we worried about our possessions. Then the train moved again and they jumped off. We kept in a close circle as the train picked up speed. A glass of water was passed and as it went from hand to hand the water danced crazily in the glass until it was nearly empty by the time it reached its supposed recipient. The professor furnished some tequila and I went back to making stew. The fireflies and the belching flame from the engine lit up the dense, jungle-like surroundings and the closeness of the stars all added up to a memorable night.

We arrived at Tapachula in the middle of the night. By now the Texans were drunk and started talking loudly about how incompetent and lazy the Mexicans were. The train employees couldn't help but hear them; we wished they would shut up but there was nothing we could do about it. They set heavy planks between the flatcars to back the autos off the train. The three autos on our flatcar went off smoothly. We thanked the rail workers and were about to drive away when we heard a lot of yelling. It seems that when the Texan's Cadillac was being unloaded the plank slipped and the car fell between the flatcars. The stevedore apologized, "We are so sorry. This has never happened before. It is a terrible thing. We are so sorry," while the Texans went on screaming. We decided it was best not to upset those whom we have to depend on and drove away to find our hotel.

The Cadillac was still there next day, resting nose down between the flatcars.

Our hotel in Tapachula was the Hotel International. It was about 3 am and the bellhop on duty was a deaf mute who made strange, loud noises, so much so that someone stuck his head out and said "Shut up!" He reminded us of Harpo Marx. He took us into the wrong room and turned on the light, which awakened a middle-aged couple. The man sat up in bed, "What the hell's going on here?" The mute made more strange noises and ushered us into another room. None of the rooms had locks. Finally we got to bed and had a good sleep.

Friday, June 26th, Tapachula, Mexico
This morning, while walking down a street of Tapachula we

heard a marimba band. We approached and listened. There were two vibraphones with one man on the base and another on the drums. The drummer's eyes stared into space through dark glasses. He continually wore a smile, which revealed his gold teeth. After finishing each number he would take out a handkerchief and gently remove the perspiration from his brown chest. The other member in sunglasses who attracted my attention did so because of his aloofness. He had no connection with either the music or the people around him, and would not smile until the number was completed. Each member changed instruments and places on the vibraphone while people came in from the street, played and left.

Lenny couldn't stand to be out of the limelight. He approached them and, after a few words and a bribe, sang. Lenny doesn't have a good voice, is not naturally musical but sings reasonably on key. The gathered crowd applauded politely, but was happy to hear the band play again.

Had my first bout with dysentery today. Mostly slept through Guatemalan customs, it took quite a while. Harvey failed to remove his hat, which the police took as an insult. They checked and rechecked his passport and papers and questioned his citizenship. We spent the night at Malacatan. I couldn't finish supper, too sick. Went to bed early. Jay also had dysentery but suffered quietly.

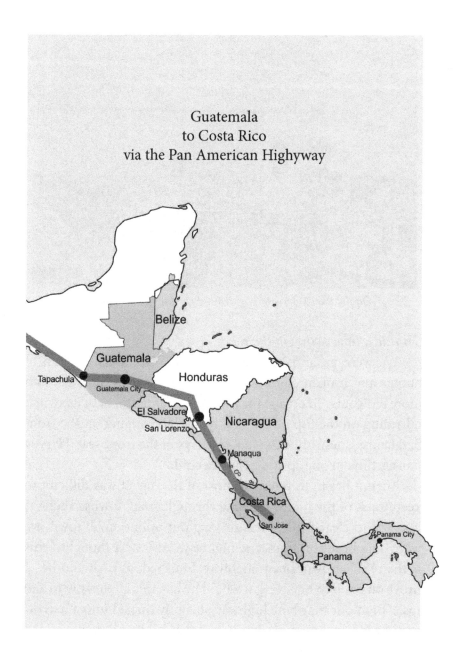

Guatemala
to Costa Rico
via the Pan American Highyway

On the Pan American Highway - Jay, stranger and Harvey

Saturday, June 27th, On the road

We were up and hit the road at six. The roads are full of bumps and broken chunks of tar. Driving is very difficult. Two more blowouts. To escape the monoxide fumes three of us switch off riding on the top of the van, lying flat, hanging on the front bar. Lenny doesn't like the top. He stays in the front seat. Harvey put his time in on top and caught a cold.

Then it began to pour for most of the day. It was difficult to keep track of the highway going through small towns. Then, as it began to clear while I was driving out of one small town, we were on a beautiful four-lane highway. "At last," I thought, "this is the real Pan American Highway. Finished, as it should be." I drove on happily, believing it would be like this all the way to San Jose. Then our four lane highway abruptly turned into a narrow gravel road that soon became a trail that led into a ravine and to a rickety bridge. A sign stuck into the ground said *pelegro* (danger). We went back to the small town and asked some questions. Seems the dictator was having a grand highway built to his home and got assassinated. So we looked around and found the rough bumpy, broken up Pan American Highway again and were on our way. I will never understand Latin America.

We drove straight through to Guatemala City arriving at 2 a.m., had a supper of cold roast beef and corn and potatoes out of cans. Our $2 hotel had straw mattresses, which were musty and dank. Harvey muttered, "This is a bad dream."

"Bad," we reassured him "but no dream."

Sunday, June 28th, Guatemala City

The drive-shaft universal joint started to rattle, which made me nervous. We decided to lay over one day to let Harvey's cold clear up a little. He is weak and in a rather depressed state. The hotel urinal overflowed and got his pants wet. Jay and I walked around town and met a Guatemalan named Jonny who works at the American Embassy. He wants to come to the States, as does everyone else we meet. He said Nicaragua is in army control. No trouble now. We will press on in the morning.

Jonny took us to the park and showed us a beautiful sculptured relief of Guatemala about eight feet square with mountains soaring up several feet.

"That's wonderful," we exclaimed. "The artist must be held in great esteem."

"No," Jonny replied. "They were afraid he would go to another country and do the same thing for them, so they had him shot." Each day brings new revelations. I am not crazy about Guatemala.

While we were in the park an old woman approached us with sugared treats for sale for the equivalent of 15 cents American. I wanted to buy some just to help her out, but Jonny drove her away saying, "She's trying to cheat you, they are not worth half that."

Back at the hotel we met three students from Duke University, John, Al and Charlie, and agreed to go to a movie with them at

9:30 pm., which gave us time for a *siesta*. Didn't see Lenny, he decided to check out of the hotel and sleep in the car.

The movie was French with Spanish sub titles. Sunday is the dress up night, suits and nice dresses. We felt out of place – Harvey in his rain poncho, Jay in his wrinkled shirt and me in travel-worn clothes. Our beards are now 20 days old. Jay's is the longest. He looks quite distinguished.

Monday, June 29th, San Salvador, El Salvador

After breakfast at the hotel we hit the road about 9 a.m., crossed the border and drove into San Salvador. Harvey wanted to stay. He had an earache, felt terrible and didn't eat all day. Unable to find a cheap hotel we continued on despite his protestations. Filthy city. We saw a man lying dead in the street but no one paid attention. We drive past 3 or 4 buildings with signs marked "*Grande Funeria*." They are dimly lit with a greenish light. In one a young boy reached down into an open coffin and then ran out the door laughing. Coffins are piled four and five high. The whole scene depressed me.

We learned not to get out our stove and cook near a town as hordes of people showed up carrying tin plates and cups. So we pulled off the road in the mountains to eat. We barely got set up when a truck driver stopped and told us to move on, "*Banditos in los montañas*." We believed him and moved on, driving most of the night. We slept in the vehicle at San Miguel.

Tuesday, June 30th, On the road

We had four flats yesterday, bringing our total count to nine. Had two that were fixable. Now down to three spares. We got off to a late start and stopped to eat by the stinking sea at San Lorenzo. Hot day. I was tired, bitchy and had a gnawing hunger since I was sick. We are filthy from the dusty Honduran roads. Harvey is feeling a little better. I know Jay is hurting but he doesn't complain. Lenny hasn't been eating local food, just Spam and canned beans. We had hoped to save them for the jungle but he makes his own decisions.

The drive-shaft universal joint is grinding more now. We plan to cross into Nicaragua in the morning, if luck is with us. Heard today there is still trouble there and we can only drive in Nicaragua during daylight.

We have now entered Honduras and are filthy from the dusty Honduran roads, the worst yet. My hair feels like a floor mat. The highway is now inland, far from the sea.

Stopped in San Lorenzo. Met an older man from New Orleans who is going by boat along the Pacific coast. Gave him a can of strawberries. People keep pointing at our beards and saying "Fidel Castro." Hope this doesn't bring political trouble. We don't want to shave.

Wednesday, July 1st, San Lorenzo, Honduras

Last night slept in the car by a bridge that was being built in Honduras by an American company. Gave the watchman a can of beans. Helped a guy catch his horse with the truck. Crossed the Nicaragua border this morning. Took some time to get the guns straightened out. Guards all over, in jeeps, on foot with tommy guns, in entrenchments in cities with machine guns. Several rebels killed last night. We get stopped constantly. Have to check in and out at each city. Had four flats today, two of them were blowouts. Tires running out. Only have six left that will hold air, three of them are very poor. Have lost count of how many flats and blowouts we've had. Hope we make it to the Costa Rican border. The drive-shaft bearing is grinding louder. We must have it repaired.

Arrived in Managua about 7:30 or 8 pm. Some guards are jumpy. As always, Jay gets us through customs with no difficulty. Takes a long time, so Jay and Lenny decide to clean their rifles in the customs office. I try to act nonchalant.

We drove around the square a half dozen times and finally found the Imperial Hotel and got two miserable rooms for $4. Beggars can't be choosers. Jay and I were in one room, Harvey and Lenny in the other. The shower was at the end of the hall but the floor was so dirty that we all showered in Jay's tennis shoes. Hot water is a luxury, haven't had it for several days. No toilet paper or towels. Toilet seat looked as though it might crawl away.

Cooked our own supper, canned chicken. Harvey and I cleaned the dishes while Jay and Lenny left to check plane fares and find out what to do about Lenny's 30-30 rifle, which is illegal in Costa Rica. Lenny will send his 30-30 rifle on to Quito. We plan to reach San Jose tomorrow, where Jay will fly on ahead to Quito and make arrangements for the mule trip across the Andes. Lenny and I will follow and Harvey will leave for Chile as soon as we dispose of the car and other equipment. I made my case for having the drive shaft universal joint repaired before leaving. It is in bad shape. We voted 3 to 1 to press on. I, the designated mechanic, was the nay vote. We turned in, somewhat apprehensive.

While Jay and I were spreading out sleeping bags over our wooden slatted cots a pretty young girl, 17 or 18, walked down the hall in a loose robe on her way to the shower. We knew she was the hotel owner's daughter. She smiled and greeted us flirtatiously, as young ladies here do. Jay and I smiled back politely, knowing an improper remark or unseemly gesture could cause trouble. Mess with her and we could all end up out on the street or tossed in jail with all of our possessions confiscated and maybe never get out. It has happened. This is Nicaragua, not Minnesota. But she was quite lovely.

Thursday, July 2nd, Managua, Nicaragua

Got away from Managua about noon. At the edge of the city soldiers stopped us and examined everything, including rifles.

They could have easily taken whatever they wanted but didn't. One had red hair.

Just outside of the city the universal joint began to clatter badly. We decided to go on as far as possible, once again I was out-voted. Fortunately they let me drive. It was 80 miles to the border and if we did not make it we would be in danger of trigger-happy soldiers as well as rebels. The clatter was less at 45 miles per hour so I kept that speed stopping only for inspections. By 4 pm we knew the frontier was near and watched carefully. I rounded a curve and saw a building on the left, no signs of any kind, so I kept moving. It was a winding, gravel road and the building did not look official. Just as we were passing the building a soldier jumped out of the front door and dropped on one knee with his tommy gun aimed at us. I slammed on the brakes. We skidded to a stop. I put my hands out the window to show I was unarmed, but couldn't get out because the driver's door was permanently welded shut. Several armed soldiers surrounded the van and ushered us out, hands over our heads. They were skittish.

After a few minutes it became clear to them that we were not rebels or any kind of a threat to them. They joked about it. "You could have gotten shot," while dropping on one knee and aiming the gun at our van. "Yes," we agreed, smiling, "we could have been shot."

The camp commandant came out and examined our papers while the soldiers tore through everything in the van. They hauled out the two rifles belonging to Jay and me. The commandant examined them and asked, "*De donde es la trenta-trenta?*" (Where is the 30-30?) Jay's Spanish was best so we let him answer.

"*No tenemos trenta-trenta.*" (We do not have a Thirty-Thirty.) He tried to tell him we had sent it on to Quito, Ecuador, from Managua. The commandant examined our papers again and said, "*De donde es la trenta-trenta?*"

"*No tenemos Trenta-Trenta,*" Jay tried again. At a gesture from the commandant the soldiers threw everything out of the van onto the ground including the seats. Then climbed up on the roof and threw down everything we had tied there, plus the spare tires. Jay asked for an interpreter. No one at the camp spoke English. The commandant had the soldiers take us inside the compound and showed us the papers where the rifle was listed as in our possession and repeated the same question over and over.

"*De donde is la trenta-trenta?*"

Jay again asks for an interpreter, but to no avail. After an hour or two of searching and questioning he let us repack the van and sent a soldier along with us to Liberia, the customs office across the frontier in Costa Rica. He was essentially done with us. The 30-30 is legal in Nicaragua but not in Costa Rica. It was now their problem.

At the Costa Rican Customs our Nicaraguan soldier explained the problem to the Lieutenant in charge, Teniente Raul Miranda Martinez, who smiled and greeted us warmly. He could afford to smile. If we were trying to pull something illegal he would arrest us and that would be it for years or a lifetime.

We found out that this compound was not just an army camp, but also the mayor's office, a police station and a prison. The lieutenant sent one of his men off with a few words, and we were escorted into a back room where we waited apprehensively. A half hour later we were returned and greeted by a small, somewhat disheveled, smiling, middle aged man, "Hi, there, you son of a bitch gringos." At last, someone who spoke the king's English! We surrounded him and told him our problem with the papers and that the gun was sent to Quito. He relayed our story to the smiling lieutenant, who began probing our story.

Meanwhile, our interpreter returned to us and talked about himself. He was Manuel Jesus Vargas, who had been arrested eleven years ago for shooting a soldier in a revolution. This he denied. He was 48, thin, with long black hair he kept tucking under his baseball hat, which he wore with the brim sharply turned upward. He was a prison fixture serving a life sentence. He took a tommy gun from one of the guards and showed us its finer points as he explained the current situation between Costa Rica and Nicaragua. He said that the Soviets furnished $100,000 worth of arms for Nicaraguan rebels, which the Costa Ricans had recovered thereby breaking up the plot. The relations between the two countries were good.

While we waited and talked with him, several young, nice looking girls came in escorted by guards, smiled at us and shimmied on to the back of the compound. Manuel grinned, obviously enjoying our puzzled looks.

"*Putas*," (prostitutes) he said. "*Putas* for the prisoners. Here they understand that even we prisoners need more than just food and water." The price was the equivalent of $1 American. We never asked where the prisoners got their money.

After rechecking it was found that the border guards had misread the papers. Jay's rifle was a .35 caliber. Mine was a .30 caliber, and Lenny's 30-30 was no longer with us. We were off the hook. It was 2 am. We gave Jesus three cans of beans and he became lively again, "I am agonna give you fellows the best meal of your days." He promptly ordered the prison cook to prepare us a chicken dinner, and started to show us around the prison.

The Lieutenant appreciated what Jesus had done but the chicken dinner was too much. Instead he offered us a cup of coffee (the most delicious I had yet tasted) accompanied by canned tuna and crackers. We all, Jesus included, sat around a large, round table and enjoyed the repast.

When the repast was over Jesus begged us to stay longer. His face looked like that of a man who had spent much time in prison. We all promised to write Manuel Jesus Vargas in care of Liberia, Costa Rica, the prison, but we never did. Before we left he slipped us a letter to mail to his sister. He said he did not like the guards reading his mail. We said we would and a guard came and led Jesus away. Teniente Raul Miranda Martinez offered to put us up for the night but we declined, not wanting to spend any more time there than necessary and left as soon as we could gracefully get away. The guard with the tommy gun smiled as we left the home of Jesus Vargas, our friend. The lieutenant handed us a letter, which would prevent any more difficulties with our guns and gave us a motorcycle escort out of town.

Friday, July 3rd, On the Road, Costa Rica

Once again we started out not knowing how long the clattering universal joint would last. I was now the designated driver because of the bad joint and kept the speed at 45 mph. Lenny was in the passenger seat as usual, as the fumes in the back bothered him. The fumes bothered Harvey and Jay too, but that was of no concern to Lenny. We were about 120 miles inside the Costa Rican border with 60 miles to go when Lenny dropped the canteen cover.

"Stop," he said. "I have to find it."

It was pitch black. "Just feel around for it, I said." He did, but without luck.

"We have to find it. We'll need this canteen in the jungle."

"Just leave it, it's not important," I replied angrily.

But he kicked up such a fuss over this nonessential that I pulled over. He found it, but that was the end of our van. It just "clunked" when I started to pull back on the highway. I crawled under. The joint was completely broken. I think we would have made it if we hadn't stopped.

So here we sat, in the middle of nowhere surrounded by trees and mountains. We decided that Jay and Lenny would hitchhike into San Jose, Jay would fly to Quito to make arrangements for our mule trip and Lenny would come back with a tow truck.

Harvey and I would wait. Fortunately a bus came by at 5:45 am and they left. Harvey and I had another look at the joint in the daylight but it was shot.

We had a chance to talk and even contemplate. The paint on the side of our van said Costa Rica or Bust. We made it over the border but would have had liked to have made it to San Jose. Now Harvey told me about an incident at the hotel in Managua. The hotel keeper's daughter that Jay and I had seen walking down the hall in her robe, carrying a towel and underclothes, caught Lenny's attention when she passed their room. Perceiving himself as a Lothario, he approached her and chatted her up. Rebuffing his advances she told him (in Spanish) that she "slept alone."

Harvey continued, "Lenny and I discussed the situation as she showered. He decided to be more aggressive. I was glad to see we had a man of action in our party. He went into the shower room in his jockey shorts and cornered her in her nighty. She fought him off. Lenny returned downtrodden. But at least he tried, that's more that the rest of us did."

I was appalled but said little about it to Harvey. He was too young to grasp the implications. Attempted rape is a serious crime in Latin America and would have involved all of us, not just the perpetrator. My anxiety increased. Did he think she was a prostitute? Or that he was so irresistible that any respectable Latin girl would yield to his advances? What was going on in his thwarted mind? Fortunately it was over. We were lucky. I didn't say anything about this to Jay, he had enough to worry about. We sang "*Cuanta La Gusta*" a couple times, talked about his female pen pal in Chile that he was eager to meet in person and had a light afternoon meal of I don't remember what. About 5:30 p.m. Lenny returned with a tow truck and a black man named Duncan.

Victor Duncan Brown claimed to be a detective and anything else that had money in it for him. Lenny had wandered about all day in San Jose without finding a tow truck. Then Duncan came up and offered his services. Said he was 59 years old. He seemed to know a lot of people and tried to get the chief of police to send out a tow truck for nothing. He tried to talk me out of my guitar and watch right away which made me leery. Why didn't Lenny go to the American Consulate? That's why they are there. Or American Express? They might know something. Now we are stuck with Victor Duncan Brown, a shyster.

The rear of our van was hoisted up. Lenny and Duncan rode in the tow truck. Harvey and I rode in the front seat of the van facing backward. The passenger side door wouldn't stay shut. I handed Harvey a rope. "Tie it to the handle and I'll secure it on my side."

"No, I'll hold it shut," Harvey said.

"I'm afraid you'll fall asleep and it will fall open."

"I won't fall asleep. It'll be fine."

It was a six-hour ride in to San Jose. He fell asleep in an hour. The door flew open and hit a new Ford truck going the other way, scratching it down the side. It was serious to be involved in an accident in Costa Rica. Duncan got into a lengthy argument, conned the other driver and we were able to continue on. Once on our way again, I tied the door shut, securely.

We stopped for a break on the way into San Jose. Harvey told Lenny that he could have half the money from the sale of the car if he would stay in San Jose and help him sell it. We had planned on staying anyway. Then they told Duncan we would give him 25% to sell it. Duncan wanted to sell it on the black market. On the ride Duncan told Lenny something about putting us in jail and scared the hell out of him. We were obligated to him, knew no one else in San Jose, and had no place to park the truck.

Once in San Jose, Duncan had the tow truck driver stop while he got a policeman to look at our van. Then he went across the street and talked to a man he called the head of Intelligence. He came back and said he would do his best to keep us out of jail.

Now all we wanted to do was unload Duncan. This was not easy. He took us to the hotel Pension Niza, which turned out to be a good hotel - good food, center of town and cheap. Lenny stayed at another hotel he had already paid for. We parked the van at Duncan's house. Harvey nicknamed him the "Black Plague."

Saturday, July 4th, San Jose, Costa Rica

Independence Day. No celebrating for us. We were six days behind our schedule, not that it meant anything. We picked up our mail at the main post office. My mother wrote that Lenny's parents had called and asked if we were still together. Lenny's letters to home said, "I went here, I went there, I ate this, I ate that, etc.," and never mentioned the rest of us. I wrote back and assured her that we were, unfortunately, still together, but in Lenny's eyes the rest of us are of no importance. I now realized that Lenny fits the textbook description of narcissism; "a pattern of traits and behaviors which signify infatuation and obsession with one's self to the exclusion of all others and the egotistic and ruthless pursuit of one's gratification, dominance and ambition." I said nothing to Jay about this but resolved to watch Lenny closely and try to keep him from getting us into serious trouble.

Harvey went to the bank to cash a traveler's check. He signed it differently than he had when he purchased the checks. The bank wouldn't cash it. This turned out to be good, however, as an English speaking man helped him out. This man had a friend in the used car business that would look at Harvey's car/truck/van. He said Duncan was a good man to sell our stuff, but not to go out with him.

Duncan took us to the police chief's house to sell our gas cans and he screwed us out of $10. We wanted to break relations but Lenny still thought he had the power to throw us in jail.

Sunday, July 5th, San Jose, Costa Rica

Duncan has the "*grippe*" and is very sick so we have a day

of rest. Harvey has diarrhea again. He was leaning out the hotel room window for some fresh air when he spotted John, Al and Charlie, the students we had met in Guatemala. We had agreed to meet them through the embassy in Costa Rica. Their bus trip ended here.

We spent the evening with them. Alan Lewis is Jewish, 18 years old and plans to become a psychoanalyst. This connects with Lenny, the soon to be psychiatrist, and the next thing I know Al wants to come with us through the jungle. Just what I needed, another student of psychology. We'll think about it.

Monday, July 6th, San Jose Costa Rica

Harvey's friend looked at the vehicle and offered him $50 plus customs, which he rejected, even though it wasn't worth that much in Minnesota.

We went to customs to find out what was involved in selling the car, then met two unsavory characters, Duncan's friends, and went with them to look at the car. While driving down the street a policeman blew his whistle at us.

"Get out quickly and walk away," the driver told us. We did. He picked us up again down the block.

"What was that about?"

"If the driver of an automobile is arrested here, they arrest everyone in the car."

Central American legal systems take some getting used to. The two of them looked at the car and our other items and agreed to meet us the next day. By now we felt we could handle Duncan and were very frank with him. He was to sell all our things, some of which were in his house, for a 10% cut. As I suspected and we later found out, he still thought the 25% deal went on the car.

Duncan lived in a slummy section of town. His two room "home" was about 8' by 15' and located deep in a tangle town. His wife was very young and very pretty. Hard for us to understand why she married him. His two small children sleep in a sheet hung over their bed. Dirt is ubiquitous. He really is poor. He always wants something (money, canned food, etc.) for his wife or kids. He had told us when we first met him he didn't live like a millionaire. This is true.

~~~

~ Part One: Arrive ~

~~~

Tuesday, July 7th, San Jose, Costa Rica

After much time consumed in going to the American Embassy, *aduanna* (customs), taking prospective buyers out to the car and just plain haggling, we finally sold the car and miscellaneous junk to Duncan's friends for about $80, (we started bargaining at $200) which went to Harvey, rightly so. (I don't know how much Lenny came away with). Buyers pay customs duty. Duncan wanted his 25%. Lenny and Harvey did a lot of bargaining and got him down to 10% by throwing in some other stuff (including my guitar). They also sold the tool kit, etc. for $11, of which I got $2. At last we are free of Duncan. Harvey's diarrhea subsided.

I talked to Alan. He comes from a wealthy, conservative Jewish family, his father is a banker. He has always had a nanny and a maid, and has never had to do anything for himself, let alone work for anyone else. Being a Jew he has a far different perspective on life and has never known want of any kind. On the other hand he is a great fan of Ayn Rand's Atlas Shrugged, which I have read and enjoyed. He hasn't read her other books, but that's okay. Atlas Shrugged is the culmination of her thoughts. We have that in common. But for clothes he only has his Brooks Brothers suit. Lenny is for Al coming along, as Al is impressed with Lenny's knowledge of psychology.

I think about it. Harvey is going to Chile. Al is 18. Maybe we need a kid to take his place. Harvey is always fun, even with diarrhea. Al seems happy and pleasant enough. Okay. We accept. Should be interesting. I had packed extra clothes, so I give Al two of my four pairs of pants and two of my four shirts. He will have to buy a pith helmet.

Things are happening fast. Now we may proceed but can only get two tickets to Panama for Wednesday (Taca airlines is running three days behind schedule) so Lenny and I hand and leg wrestled to see who goes with Al (Charlie had his own ticket). I won, as usual. Lenny likes to contest for everything and always loses. He and Harvey will follow on Thursday.

Can't help noticing that the girls in San Jose are very pretty, second only to Mexico City. We are all happy to be finished with the arduous trip through Central America. Harvey will stay with a poor family in Chile. I look forward to a pleasant mule ride over the Andes. Throughout my childhood I had farmer friends with horses and enjoyed riding. Mules walk stiff legged and are said to be less comfortable to ride but they can't be that much different just walking on a trail, can they? We'll find out. Lenny has said nothing about the mule trip; be interesting to see how he does. Al is young enough and small enough to endure physical rigors even though he is not at all athletic. Jay and I will just do it and enjoy the adventure.

Wednesday, July 8, 1959 Panama City

Panama was in a state of unrest. The four of us had an arduous trip through Central American revolutions without serious incident. We were no threat to either side and accepted being regularly checked by local police and armies as a way of life. Latin American revolutions are, for the most part casual, with sudden spurts of shootings, burnings and riots that seldom accomplish anything. Al, Charlie and John had traveled through the same countries by bus without any problems. But in January, Panama had experienced serious rioting and bloodshed (a couple dozen dead) about the control of canal and country. The canal zone was American, they wanted it back. Tensions were still high.

Charlie, Al and I flew to Panama City for $25 each, on Taca International Airlines, only to find that we had a three-day layover before flying to Quito. Taca was running behind schedule. It cost $7 to take a taxi into Panama City. Our room at the Pension Residential with a light breakfast cost $4. The Pension Niza in San Jose cost $3 a day including meals. Panama City was more expensive. When Lennie, Harvey and Dan came on Thursday, they moved into the Pension Alfaro, run by the sister-in-law of the man who owned the Pension Residencia. We joined them.

This was our chance to see the city individually. Lenny bought a white suit and handed Al his movie camera to record him strutting for posterity. Lenny will have different trip stories to tell than the rest of us. I bought a couple hot dogs from a street vendor. Al didn't, they might contain pork but he noticed the lettuce on mine didn't look good. I had already eaten one. I pulled the lettuce out of the remaining one and found a long green worm. Panamanians did not like Americans and found creative ways of making this evident, even mocking us walking down the street.

Charlie and I walked into a park to avoid some street youths. A young man, who seemed to like gringos, joined us.

"You get used to it," he said. "They most likely won't attack you physically but the country is in revolution and it could get nasty again." We just listened. "Latin America has never been stable, first robbed and exploited by Spain and Portugal and now by the United States."

I protested, but he went on. "Our laws and governments are set up and controlled by whom? United Fruit? Rubber companies? The CIA? Huge corporations? We don't really know because they support the various families who rule countries such as the Samosas in Nicaragua."

"Yes, I know," I said. "I spent a night in jail there."

"You were lucky to get away," he continued. "If things go well, peace prevails. If not, the powers that be replace one ruling family with another. Usually no one is shot. After a big show of force the first family goes off to Europe or America to spend the contraband they have accumulated. They may come back in a few years. Bolivia has had a revolution every year of its existence. Nothing changes."

He offered us a cigarette and lit up himself. "How different if the English had colonized us. We would have law, order and a stable currency with our own justice system in place." He exhaled deeply, blowing smoke into the air. "Yes," he said, "we would have the basis for our independence. Now we have to start building from anarchy and chaos." He shook his head sadly and snubbed his cigarette. "Enjoy your stay," he said, smiled and left.

"Gives us some idea of what's going on," Charlie offered. "This stranger might be somebody someday," I said.

"Yes, he might, but we will never know, having no idea who he is."

We continued walking casually down the street when a limousine pulled up. Someone rolled down the window and asked if we wanted to tour the town. It was Al. We got in, soon found Harvey and had a pleasant afternoon taking a chauffeured tour of the city. Later, back at the pension, I asked Al, "How the hell did you pull that off?"

"I just went down the street until I found a shop with a Jewish name, walked in and said 'Shalom.'"

"He's been doing this the whole trip," Charlie said.

It must be nice, I thought, to have an international identity. I was curious to know more about Al. His life so far as I knew consisted of school, family and his Bar Mitzvah. The next big event was a cousin's wedding in September. He planned to spend the next six years in school and become a Freudian psychoanalyst. "I'm going to make a fortune off neurotic old Jewish ladies." He loved Ayn Rand's philosophy of acquisition and domination.

~~~

Part Two:
Over the Andes in Ecuador by Mule

~~~

~ Plan ~

~~~

Sunday, July 12, Quito, Ecuador

Al and I saw Harvey off to Chile on Saturday and flew to Quito on Sunday. Jay met us at the airport and took us to his boarding house, the Residencia Giovanna and introduced us to his new friend Carlos who announced airplane flights in English and Spanish at the airport. Carlos acted as his interpreter.

In Minnesota Jay had listened to the Quito missionary station, HCJB, on shortwave radio. Once here he contacted them for information and they referred him to Rachael Saint, whose husband was one of the five missionaries killed by the Aucas in 1956.

The world knew nothing about the savage Aucas until the mid-twentieth century as the Aucas had always killed anyone who had seen them and frequently murdered members of their own tribes. The total number left in the three tribes was less than 600. One young woman, Dayuma, whose family had been murdered, "given the spear," by other tribal members, managed to escape and was taken in by a missionary group. Rachael Saint was learning the language from her and composing a dictionary when her husband and the four others decided to make contact with the tribe. This resulted in their deaths, which became international news.

Quito, Ecuador - Residencia Giovanna - Loading up for mule trip
Pepe Castro (drover, seated), Jay, Jack, Lenny, Al

Pepe Castro, Lenny, Jay, Carlos, onlookers

Two years later Rachael, brave soul that she was, went into Auca territory and managed to live with them carrying on the missionary work. They tolerated her, thinking she was looking for a husband.

This was not comforting information. We would be traveling through Auca territory and I didn't think looking for a wife would be enough of an excuse to save our lives. But as Jay said, "These things happen to other people, not us." First we had to get over the Andes. Rachael told Jay how to make contact with Pepe Castro, a mule drover, for the trip across the Andes. He lived in Tumbaco, 10 miles east of Quito. Jay had made the trip with Carlos as an interpreter. They rode the rail-bus, a bus fitted with train wheels that drove on tracks, to Tumbaco and made arrangements for our trip across the Andes from Tumbaco to Tena on the Napo River. *Señor* Castro was to collect us in Quito, July 15th.

This left us a couple days to see Quito and buy additional supplies. Jay, Al, Carlos and I climbed the mountain overlooking the city and viewed the surrounding mountain peaks. Beautiful, but I couldn't fully enjoy the scenery. I was too intent on the mule trip. Lenny went off on his own. We talked to other missionaries who praised Castro but said it was a difficult and often dangerous journey. "Once over the Andes," they added, "you'll probably lose some or all of your supplies on the trip downriver. Camp only on the left side of the Napo River, the Aucas live on the right." However, none of them had crossed the Andes by mule or taken a dugout canoe down the river. They flew in on missionary airplanes and used Pepe Castro to haul supplies in for them.

Quito was a romantic city, from the sound of its name to the streets filled with its colorful people. Numerous shops, some with doors on the street and others that can be entered only after going down alleys and up dark stairways into dimly lighted cubicles, offered everything from shrunken heads to precious stones. That is, if you knew the "right people." But you can find the "right people" on almost any street corner. We went from shop to shop and haggled, not our style, but the custom. If you pay the price asked they are disappointed, but if you haggle they are happy because they got every cent they could squeeze out of you. We bought soap, mirrors and salt to trade, and ponchos and bread cakes for us, plus a 10-pound tin of hard biscuits that we planned to dole out, two biscuits per man per day.

I was concerned because we had few canned goods left to last us a month in the Oriente. "We'll eat what the natives eat," Jay said, always optimistic. We had no idea what the natives ate or if they would trade with us, but we had three rifles and a 22 caliber pistol. We hoped to hunt. Fact is we had no idea what we were getting into.

One evening as we sat on the veranda while the moon, full and bright, danced off the neighboring rooftops, all was quiet, save for a mother singing softly to her crying child. Time, seemingly, did not exist. A slight breeze stirred and caressed us into tranquility. Then an Ecuadorian man who was also staying at the Residentia Giovanna interrupted our serenity. After exchanging greetings in Spanish he said,

"I hear you are going into the Oriente."

"That is correct," Jay answered in Spanish.

"It is very dangerous, many do not return."

"But don't padres and settlers live there?"

"Si, a few along the river, but there are savage indios, Jivaros and Aucas, who shrink your head to the size of your fist (he held up his closed fist) and eat you."

"But many have been there,"

"Si, and many have died. There are insects that can kill a man with one bite, snakes that strangle you, *tigres* (jaguars) that …" At this point our informant was on his feet waving his arms and predicting death for at least one of us. When questioned, he admitted he had never been in the jungle, but "had heard." After he had delivered his message he said, "*Buenos noches,*" gravely and left.

An Ecuadorian girl at the University of Minnesota had said the same to Jay, "The jungle will claim you." She too had never been in the jungle but "had heard." Quito is merely 100 miles from the Oriente but these people knew less than we did. We were determined to find out for ourselves. I was apprehensive, but the danger made it enticing.

I tried to make sure all was in order. Carlos called me the "mother hen," clucking around and flapping his elbows up and down. He also made fun of Lonnie. Breakfast came with *café con leche*, strong coffee to which we added milk and sugar. Carlos mimicked Lennie, pouring coffee, adding milk and sugar, tasting, again and again, finally pushing it aside and not drinking it. We all laughed, except Lenny. I liked Carlos; he had a sense of humor. One morning we were served scrambled eggs mixed with an unfamiliar rubbery substance. Jay asked Carlos "What kind of meat is this?" Carlos had to think a minute to remember the English word. Then he pointed to his head and said, "Brains. Calves brains." Jay's mouth stopped in mid chew pondering whether to spit them out or swallow. Then years of "Minnesota nice" came through. He smiled, swallowed hard and reached for another forkful.

Tuesday, July 14, Quito

Lenny told us he had visited a doctor and found out that he had the symptoms of malaria. He then went off for the day. Al, Jay and I packed our stuff. Would we ever use our dutch oven or the Coleman gas camping stove? Did we need them? *Quien sabe?* (Who knows?) But we packed them, just in case, along with the vitamin pills recommended by my pharmacist friend which none of us had taken before. Food would be a problem, as we had no way to carry eggs and bread. Eggs cost one *sucre* each, seven and a half cents, and bread a *sucre* a loaf. In Minnesota a dozen eggs cost about the same as a loaf of bread. We each bought two loaves of bread with hard crusts figuring they would hold up.

Lenny returned to the pension that night complaining of

chills, fever and flu-like symptoms, the text book definition of malaria, and said he couldn't go with us on Wednesday. He had to see the doctor again and also check on his rifle, but would tough it out and join us on Thursday in time for the mules. Jay and I thought he looked well enough. We couldn't postpone the mule trip, it would mean a months delay.

Wednesday, July 15. Quito – Tumbaco

Lenny joined us for breakfast, mentioning that he might also have hepatitis. He planned to spend the day in bed but surely would join us in Tumbaco tomorrow, as he would hate to miss the mule ride over the Andes. Carlos said he would look after Lenny and help him get on his way.

Castro arrived and we bade goodbye to Lenny, Carlos and the other residents of the Residencia Giovanna who bid us *adios* (goodbye) instead of *hasta la vista* (until we next meet), sure it was for the last time. We had so much baggage to haul to the rail-bus that it barely fit in the taxi. The 10-mile bus ride on train tracks was comfortable and made me wonder why these vehicles weren't more prevalent. The Mountains filled with trees were spectacular, the timber line here must be 20,000 feet.

Once we arrived in Tumbaco, Castro had our luggage taken to an adobe hut and walked us three miles to his house, a large, ramshackle, two story building in a clearing, a remnant from a more prosperous time. We wondered why such a large house had no glass in the windows, but realized that none of the buildings in Tumbaco, had glass windows. Not needed? Too expensive?

Pepe's seven children greeted us warmly and happily danced around, and gave us parched corn on tin plates. As guests to these hospitable people we dutifully chewed away at this tasteless field corn that we would only feed to cattle. It was all they had to offer. This was the noon meal.

The house was bare except for two chairs brought for us.

Where were the beds? Upstairs? Did they have beds or just sleep on the floor? Dirt covered all, inside and out, but his family had shelter from the elements. The adobe kitchen, separated from the building, had a fire on the dirt floor with a large pot over it. His smiling wife was tending the pot and fire. She greeted us but did not speak.

This was our first personal contact with real poverty except for Duncan's hovel in San Jose. Castro had income from his mules and was able to feed his family but they would envy the poorest of the poor in the States.

Pepe Castro walked us back to the adobe hut in Tumbaco and threw a straw mattress on the floor. A lizard darted for the window. Al was after it but Castro waved him off indicating they eat insects. Do we choose to sleep with lizards or insects? Both, it turned out.

Castro's dialect was difficult to understand, but we guessed we would leave for Papallacta at 6 am *mañana*. The village, Papallacta, "just over the pass," sounded promising. Perhaps a nice warm meal with meat and a bed awaited us, instead of a filthy floor.

Supper was served at the adobe hut next door – *locro*, (a thin potato soup) coffee and a small portion of rice. This left us wanting, but we had vowed to "eat what the natives eat." We smiled and thanked the cook.

The small hut was crowded with our baggage and other debris. The mattress was too small so we decided to zip two sleeping bags together on the dirty floor and use the mattress for a pillow. I lost the coin toss and had to sleep in the middle. We scrunched down to avoid crawling insects and went to sleep thinking of the adventurous mule trip ahead.

Thursday, July 16, Tumbaco

The next morning Castro, who had gone home for the night, woke us at daybreak, which was always at 6 a.m. near the equator. Jay and I had blood spots on our arms and thought vampire bats caused them because they were small wounds. *Señor* Castro glanced at them and said *moscos*, mosquitoes. "Must be damn big *moscos*," we thought. Vampire bats, contrary to popular belief, do not suck blood from their victims, but make a wound and lick the blood from it. The danger is the diseases they carry, including rabies. They return to the same victim night after night until he dies. This happens to animals and humans. We watched the bites for the next few days. They healed. Either they were *moscos* or the bats couldn't find us again because we were on the move.

It was cold, windy and drizzling rain. We rolled up our sleeping bags, put on what heavy clothes we had, slipped into our ponchos and followed Castro, to meet the mules.

"*Hoy Papallacta, mulos mañana,*" (Today papallacta, mules tomorrow) he said, as he and his helper threw our bags into a flatbed homemade vehicle, a new truck chassis with wooden benches along the sides in the back, cramped seating for maybe 12 people. No mules today? It was confusing but we were in his hands. The front section had two benches; the first was for the driver, his mechanic and the three of us. The bench just behind us sat six. This vehicle had no roof.

We scrunched up in our sweaters and ponchos and got as comfortable as possible for the rainy cold ride over the crest. We had no idea where we were or how far it was to Papallacta. The mechanic's job was to fix whatever went wrong and get us out of any difficulty. When he snubbed his cigarette out on the shiny dash, I knew this vehicle would not appear new for long. Fourteen passengers piled onto the benches in the back with chickens, crates of animals and miscellaneous sacks. We set off.

Lenny hadn't showed, which didn't surprise me. Castro was gone, we knew not where and had no idea what route he and his mules were taking to Papallacta.

The miserable rain streamed down as we gained altitude.

"Jay, how high are we?" Al asked.

"A little over 10,000 feet."

"How high is Papallacta?"

"Just under 13,000, but the pass between is 16,000."

"Will we be staying in a hotel in Papallacta?"

"We won't know till we get there."

Al hadn't quite grasped that Papallacta was a poor, dirty mountain village on a rugged trail traveled by few people. I had no desire to get into this cheerful conversation, as I too, wanted to believe a hotel was waiting for us.

The road was rough, rutty and bumpy as we began and soon got worse – muddy ruts. Jay asked the mechanic, in Spanish, "How far is it to Papallacta?"

"Only 65 kilometers," he answered with a casual flick of his hand. Forty miles. No big deal, just a short trip. I did some calculating. It was 115 kilometers from Tumbaco to Tena, according to our map. Subtracting 65 kilometers from that makes our mule trip only 50 kilometers, roughly 30 miles. "Ah," I thought, "that's nothing. Piece of cake. Two days by mule, three at most."

The weather turned colder. I pulled my hat down tighter, hunched into my poncho and sat shivering. I looked at my companions. Jay smiled. Al smiled. The passengers in back with only thin clothing were enduring. It's their world. I was suffering but decided not to complain, as I had no one to complain to. We climbed higher on the narrow, twisting trail. It started to snow. Snow! Thirty miles from the equator! Surprisingly Al was ecstatic, catching snowflakes in his hand. He had never seen snow before. This cheered me a little.

We came to a mud-hole covering the entire width of the road. The driver stopped the bus and his assistant got out to survey the situation. After a heated discussion, which everyone in the bus joined in except us, it was decided to plow through it. I would have voted for more examination, but my Spanish was limited. Unfortunately the hole was deeper than expected and the bus dropped in and stuck fast. Simply sticking a pole in the hole would have showed it's depth, but that's not the way they did things here. Just gun the engine and plow through.

Everyone got out and unloaded the baggage and animals. Everyone but Al, who sat tight. "We're paying customers, it's their job to see we get there." Jay and I just smiled; Al would always do as little as possible. We were going to help but changed our mind after watching the driver's helper, knee deep in mud, trying to jack up the bus with no solid footing for the jack.

The snowstorm blew into a blizzard. It was impossible to see more than 10 feet. Surprising, even at 15,000 feet, I thought. The other passengers, wearing only ponchos, light shirts, knee length pants and sandals didn't seem to be cold. We, in heavier clothing, were freezing. Everyone got back on the bus and most of them promptly went to sleep. A skinny old lady aged 40 or 45, (people age fast in the Andes) came trudging up the road through the mud and snow with a big bundle on her back. She was barefoot and the first person we saw that looked cold. We gave her one of our seats on the bus, and Jay and I took turns standing out in the snow.

The helper gave up on the jack after a few hours, walked off and came back with a long pole. Then, finding a suitable rock for leverage, tried to pry the truck onto solid ground. He obviously needed help with this so Jay and I, along with three other men, put our weight on the lever. The truck moved a few inches. We reset the rock, levered again and moved a few more inches, again and again. To make a long, miserable story short we finally got the truck onto somewhat solid ground. I glanced at my $5 Timex watch, which had survived the rain, mud, snow and cold and realized we had been there five hours! Five hours stuck in a mud hole in a blizzard 30 miles from the equator. Again I wanted to complain but the other passengers threw their luggage back on and were ready to go. Jay didn't complain, it's not his style. Al didn't complain. He was still trying to get a good look at the snowflakes that kept melting on him. I resolved, when I got back to Minnesota, I would tell my friends what a real blizzard feels like.

Our duffles were soaked and heavier than six hours earlier. The chickens seemed okay in their wooden crates. I thought of Pepe Castro leading his mules through this storm to Papallacta, but knew he would be fine. The old lady we rescued moved to the back benches to be closer to her bundle. The driver never charged her. One old man pleaded pathetically for someone to throw his clump of belongings on the truck, as it was too heavy for him. They all ignored him. He was on his knees in the mud, pleading, when Jay and I threw his stuff on. This was a tough world with little pity or Christian charity.

It felt wonderful to be moving again though our shoes were muddy, our feet wet and our bodies cold and hungry. But I thought it is good for us gringos to experience this other world. Fact is I was miserable and had experienced enough of the other world. We made it over the pass and were on a downhill run, clipping along this rough, bumpy trail at 15 to 20 miles per hour. We would soon be in Papallacta. I scrunched up and fell asleep.

We did not yet know that in this world disaster could strike any minute. The truck came to an abrupt stop, jarring me awake. I looked up and saw the road was gone. What were we doing driving into a pile of rocks? I turned, looked back and saw the road was still there. A landslide had completely covered the road ahead to a depth of four or five feet. The driver's helper didn't get out. No need. Nothing that he could do would free us.

We waited. The driver and his mechanic-helper got into another animated conversation and the helper took off down the mountainside. We waited.

"Why don't they do something?" Al said.

"Like what?" Jay asked.

"Clear the road and get us on our way."

Al was still in Alabama. I chose not to explain to him that there wasn't a backhoe or bulldozer handy and if there were it would take hours, maybe days, to reopen the road.

We waited. Finally, after an hour and a half, the helper reappeared with several people from Papallacta to tote our luggage. It was a three-mile miserable trudge through mud and some of our bags were heavy, especially the knapsack filled with books, which we hadn't yet opened. Al, begrudgingly, now had to disembark and walk.

We had six duffle bags plus sleeping bags and other supplies. A young man and his wife carried two, she the heavy one with books and he a lighter one with clothes. We carried some of the sleeping bags and a few personal items. The young wife helped her husband with his lighter bag as much as possible; women are better at toting than men. They were both chewing what we later found out were coca leaves, the source of cocaine. Some natives stay high most of their lives. As we trudged down the steep, muddy, miserable path, I envied their coca leaves.

It was dark when we reached Papallacta. We toked the carriers and once again were destined to sleep on the floor of a dirty shack, a room in the commissary's office. Supper was a real treat, *locro*, rice, coffee and, glory be, small chunks of beef. Not a substantial meal, but enough to placate our hunger, somewhat.

Jay managed to find a telephone and called the pension in Quito. Carlos told him that Lenny claimed to have both malaria and hepatitis, but couldn't come to the phone; he was out on the town. He didn't seem sick to Carlos but said he would meet us in Tena. We now knew that Lenny was faking it to avoid the mule trip. I hoped he really would fly back to the states. At least now we were free of him for the mule trip.

What in hell was I doing here? I could be sleeping in a nice warm bed in Minnesota with a belly full of food and not have to worry about anything. But this was an adventure and while I was not happy to be here now, I thought I shall some day be pleased for the experience of having been here. At least that's what I told myself.

Our shack was crammed full of gear so we again decided to zip two sleeping bags together for the three of us. Again I lost the coin flip and got the middle. We took off our wet clothes, crawled into the sleeping bags and went to sleep.

Friday, July 17, Papallacta

Next morning after putting on semi-dry clothes we found Castro who told us that we could not leave today, a *puente* (bridge) had washed out. We would start *mañana*, 6 am.

The local restourante served us rice, a piece of fried dough and small chunks of beef with delicious coffee. It seems our trip included bed and breakfast, but rarely a bed. And sometimes no breakfast. Over coffee we tried to figure out how they could put up a bridge in one day. We may be here for many *mañanas*.

Castro started bumming cigarettes every time we lit up, which was often. We might run out before Iquitos, Peru. We had stocked up on Winstons. The Ecuadorian cigarettes smelled bad and tasted worse. We should have purchased some for Castro. We didn't know how to say "no" to him. In his mind, gringos had endless wealth and a few cigarettes more or less would make no difference.

Papallacta houses are not made of adobe but of wood, are raised off the ground on stilts and have grass roofs and window holes. In the clear blue sky the scenery was a beautiful, mountain peak turning purple fading off into the distance. We spent the day keeping warm and watching the mule drovers, *arrieros*, get ready for the trip. We had pooled our money for expenses and agreed to give Castro 800 *sucres*, about a hundred dollars, when we reached Tena on the Napo River. Jay believed this was much more than he would charge locals, but he was so poor we didn't begrudge him the money and knew he would look out for us. His trip over and back would take nearly a month.

The village residents told us, near as we could comprehend, that it rains daily, the trail gets worse after Cuyuja, is bad into Baeza then worse again until Archidona, which is only eight miles from Tena, our destination.

Jay and I bought 10 eggs and three loaves of bread and decided to fry our last can of Spam for a final meal before the mule trip. We pumped up the Coleman gas stove and got out the cast iron frying pan. I opened the Spam, noticed it didn't go psst when I turned the key, but thought it wouldn't matter if we fried it. Al hadn't paid attention until he saw the Spam.

"Spam has pork in it. I can't eat pork."

"Surely the Rabbi will let you break the dietary law under unusual circumstances," I said.

"No. I'll have the tuna."

"That's our last can. We were saving that for the mule trip."

"I can't eat pork."

He was adamant so we all had scrambled eggs and bread, Al with tuna, Jay and I with Spam. We turned in contented with a full belly.

An hour or two later Jay crawled out of the sleeping bag and ran for the door. I could hear him vomiting and couldn't help but laugh. I was soon back asleep. Then I awoke, my stomach churning in pain, crawled out of the bag and ran in the dark for the wood slat door, hitting it with both elbows only to find it locked. I was standing in and vomiting on Jay's puke. Our keepers had locked us in so no one could steal our supplies. After several heaves I scraped off my feet and crawled back in the sleeping bag. Our dented can of Spam had gone bad. Al slept calmly through the ordeal. Ah, to be a Jew.

Mule Trip over the Andies

~~~
~ Part Two: Travel ~
~~~

Saturday, July 18, Papallacta to Cuyuja

Some unknown kind person had cleaned the mess before we awoke. Our mule caravan was gathering, 29 mules, one horse and six drovers, lean rugged men in ragged clothes with sandals made from discarded car tires. The mules' backs were red, rubbed raw from the saddles and packs. They rolled in the grass whenever possible. A difficult life for man and mule, I thought.

We were about to enter the Oriente, the Province of the Oriente, an area the size of New York and New England together on the eastern slope of the Ecuadorian Andes. Both Peru and Ecuador have disputed ownership for over 100 years. The area we planned to travel through on a 400-year-old trail between the Marañon River and its tributary the Putumayo, is known as Napo country. Earlier, the Conquistadores came through bringing smallpox and other diseases to some five million Napos, Zaparos, Jivaros and other tribes that inhabited the land. Now there are but a few thousand left.

It would not have helped if someone had told us to "pick your mule carefully, you will be together for the nine most wretched, miserable, wet, cold, hungry, bone-jarring, bug-bitten days of your life." No, it would not have helped. We had no choice. *Señor* Pepe Castro simply slapped three of his scroungy animals on the rear and introduced them by name as they ambled toward us. Then, without ceremony that ended with the solemn words "I now pronounce you man and mule," we were wedded, so to speak: Jay with Adelante (onward), Al with Resuelta (determined) and I with Enduro (Endure). Enduro, my mount, was an old sway-backed nag of a horse. I patted him on the neck to introduce myself in a friendly fashion, but he was too old and worn out to respond. He, like many humans in similar circumstances, took the path of least resistance, got in line and did his duty.

The other mule drovers, Garson in center

These were pack animals. We did not ride them, just sat on them. No bridle, just a halter. They followed the mule tail ahead, whether carrying passengers or baggage. I imagined that some-day someone would ask me what the scenery was like in the An-des. "Scenery is the rear end of the mule just ahead of you," I vowed to glibly reply. Sometimes a quick glance upward revealed beautiful blue sky, clouds, mountain peaks, trees and birds. Ex-hilarating! But mostly we struggled to stay on the rough, rocky trail, ducking under tree branches which scratched neck and ears, tried to put eyes out and were sometimes low enough to wipe you clean out of the saddle.

I had ridden horseback as a kid so I knew how to neck rein, which was no help here as there were no reins, just a rope around the animals neck to the halter. We just sat and ducked. And the saddles? Wood. Rough wood, which pinched if one didn't keep all appurtenances in place and sit with caution. It was not so bad this first day for me on the horse but our unions were not permanent. Castro gave us a different animal everyday. Still, as we mounted up we thought it would be an easy, peaceful ride on sure footed animals ambling over an old trail through magnificent mountain scenery. This was our chance to rest up and prepare for the arduous, dangerous trip down river through the jungle.

Al, on Resuelta

Mules on the mountain trail

Jay and Al ambling through bramble

It was raining. The bridge indeed, was out; the whole mountainside had washed away. Nothing but a flood of water six inches to two feet deep poured over the half football field width we had to cross. Perhaps the drovers had thought it would rain less today and be safer but that was not to be. It was dangerous. One misstep and man and beast would cascade over the side of the mountain. The other five drovers were waiting by the river as we approached. After an arm waving heated discussion they came to a consensus and started to cross. As each mule hesitated at the edge he was given a swat and plunged in. We were the only riders, all the rest were pack animals. The drovers walked.

We had purchased six loaves of bread and each had one left. I had no place to carry mine, so, needing both hands for balance, I gave it to *Señor* Castro. He thanked me profusely, "*Mucho gras, mucho gras.*" I thought he was overdoing it but two days later, hungry, I wished I had taken the trouble to carry it myself.

I could feel Enduro moving one foot at a time, making certain it was secure before putting weight on it and then slowly moving another foot. He had been through it all before and didn't want to go over the side of the mountain anymore than I did. Still, I wished I were on a mule, they were better at this. One misstep could mean death to man and beast. After an arduous step-by-step process, we made the 150 feet across to solid ground. Did I mention it was raining? Ponchos kept upper body dry but our legs were soaked. I couldn't help feeling sorry for myself until I noticed the drovers, dressed in ragged loose clothing, soaked to the skin, gently urging their mules along.

This 400 year old trail, the same that had been used by Francisco de Orellano, the first European to cross the Andes, was narrow and full of serpentine twists and turns between trees. We pressed on. We could not talk without shouting so we didn't. I thought our crossing the washout was the only difficulty and the rest of the ride would be easy, despite the rain. Not to be. Our drovers halted again. We looked up and saw that the majestic mountainside ahead had fallen away. Twenty to 30 feet of thick topsoil had come loose and slid down the mountain. We were staring at a 45 degree slope of black dirt.

"Well, that's the end of our mule trip, we'll never get around that," I said. But I had underestimated the natives who had been using the trail for the past 300 years. Several men were already at work with machetes. Machetes! In a short time they had hacked a foot wide trail out of the black dirt and we followed Pepe Castro across it leading our animals, expecting the earth to give way and drop us a thousand feet onto the rocks below. I hugged the mountainside with both arms, loosely leading Enduro, not wanting to hang on to him if he slipped. However, if I slipped I would hang on to the rope around his neck. It was every horse for himself, so to speak. We made it and I felt relieved to once again be on the solid trail.

I would not do something like this on a bet or a dare, even to save my pride. It was dangerous and foolhardy, but we all did it without hesitation. We had no choice. Jay and I were glad and relieved to have made it. Al was smiling, enjoying the adventure. I envied his mindset.

"We certainly have had a rough first day so far, but the rest of the trip should be better," I said, once again tempting the Viking gods who pounce on the weaknesses of their adherents.

On we plodded through the driving rain with seldom a chance to dismount. Our boots were wet and muddy. Mules follow the tail ahead of them, mostly. We, in Castro's group of five mules and a horse, brought up the rear of the caravan. One of our mules decided not to follow the tail ahead of her, but to take the nigher route through a large puddle. It turned out to be a mud-hole. In she went, up to the withers. By the time I got there, Castro was in the hole with the mule, trying to push and coax her out. I laughed at the stupid mule and went on over the crest to where to Jay and Al were, off their mules, standing in their shining, rain drenched ponchos.

"Did you see that stupid mule?" I said.

Jay laughed. "Show Jack," he said to Al.

Al, still smiling, lifted up his poncho to reveal his whole body covered with mud.

"That was Al's mule," Jay said.

He could have taken off his poncho and let the rain wash the mud off his clothes, but he didn't. Just stood there smiling.

Castro got Resuelta out, packed her and saddled another mule, Piqueño, (small) for Al. Resuelta did the same thing 30 feet along down the trail, this time getting our packs wet. Castro, normally a reserved man, shouted out a string of wonderfully expressive expletives that I wish I knew. I dug my heels into Enduro's flanks to get away before Castro put me on Resuelta.

After many hours of slogging through mud in a pouring rain we arrived at Cuyujua, a small village consisting of a few homes, some adobe, some wood, all with blackened grass roofs from smoke. Our table was set with bowls. Jay wrote his name in the sand in his bowl before the soup was ladled, a wasted effort, our Quechua hostess couldn't read. It didn't matter, we could never eat the last of the soup anyway, the river water it was made from was too sandy. The buns were gray and gritty to chew. Hunger alters one's partiality considerably. A little rice with a fried egg on top rounded off our meal, our only meal of the day. I had a yearning for a nice piece of steak "smothered in onions," as Laurel and Hardy used to say.

Our first day on the mules left us wet, worn out and miserable. The good news was that Castro said we are four days out of Napo, just beyond Tena. At least that's what we understood. My calculations of two days were wrong, but four days would still be great.

All Andean villages are near streams. Cuyuja had an outhouse of sorts, an open, grass-roofed small floor on stilts, with two holes over the stream. Just aim and squat. Fortunately, the lady who makes the soup lives upstream.

Our shelter was a grass-roofed shanty. We slept on the floor in our sleeping bags. Jay and I draped our clothes over the open windows to dry. Al threw his muddy clothes in a corner. Castro and another drover slept in the same shack with us and, as always, bummed cigarettes. They had only thin blankets. I think I would rather make Popsicles the rest of my life than run mules like Castro does. But maybe the life suits him. Maybe he likes working with mules, or maybe he has little choice. I vaguely remembered a quote from Darwin "That a hybrid mule should possess more reason, memory, obstinacy, social affection, powers of muscular endurance, and length of life than either of its parents, seems to indicate that art has here outdone nature." I don't think Darwin had ever ridden a mule. They have these characteristics but are the very devil to ride.

We each had two biscuits from our ten-pound tin. I wanted to write every detail of our day in my logbook, but Jay wanted the candle out so he could sleep.

Sunday, July 19. Cuyuja to Baeza

"I need another shirt and a pair of pants, these are too muddy to wear," Al said as he climbed out of the sleeping bag and picked up his wet clothes in the corner.

"I don't have any more," I said.

"You said you'd supply me with clothes," he declared testily.

"I said I would give you half of mine, two pairs of pants and two shirts. That's all I have. Where are the other ones I gave you?"

"They were dirty so I threw them."

Al was used to having everything provided for him by a mammy and a maid and had never had to manage for himself. I wasn't about to give him my last pair of pants, the ones I had on already had a rip in them.

"You'll have to wear the clothes you wore on the bus through Central America. What's wrong with them?"

"That's my Brooks Brothers suit. I can't wear that out here."

I shrugged my shoulders. He looked at Jay who also had no clothes to spare. Jay shrugged. Al looked again at his muddy pants and shirt lying in the corner and reluctantly dug out his Brooks Brothers suit. Once dressed he looked neat and spiffy in his tailored pants and jacket. He may be the first man to cross the Andes by mule in a Brooks Brothers suit, I thought. I suggested we get a picture of him on Piqueño and send it to the Brooks Brothers Company in New York for advertising. Al did not think it was funny. To him fine clothes were not a joking matter.

Breakfast was rice and an egg with a piece of fried dough. This, and coffee, was standard fare. Pepe Castro bestowed upon me the honor of riding Resuelta, herself who had dumped Al in the mud, even after I had given him my last loaf of bread. I suppose better me in the mud than the cargo. I was prepared to dismount at a moment's notice. Poor swayed back Enduro carried a heavy load of our supplies. A distressing sight but he would endure until he died on the trail. Pack animals are not "put out to stud" like race horses.

The sun was shining, a nice breeze blew the bugs away, the

Andes peaks looked beautiful, birds flew overhead. I prognosticated: "Today will be the first in a series of pleasurable rides."

Resuelta made several circles before deciding to join the cavalcade. She had her own way of doing things and with only a single rope tied to her neck there was nothing I could do about it. We were the last in line of the thirty mules Resuelta nearly scraped me off a couple times, on low branches. Not on purpose, I thought, but she may be more devious than I gave her credit for. Mules have two gaits, a slow stiff-legged, bone-jarring walk and a slightly faster stiff-legged bone-jarring walk. Sitting in a wooden saddle on a buoyant mule made me rethink the purpose of life, but philosophizing in such conditions quickly passes from the mental to the physical, from the head to the rear end.

It was another day of fording rivers and leading the mules around dangerous, narrow paths, but we were becoming acclimated. Baeza, our destination, is a village over 300 years old. James Orton, who had taken this same route in 1866, described it in his book, Andes and the Amazon. Except for an increase in population it had changed little. I felt we were meeting the same natives he had described. Baeza was a village of 100 to 150 people centered on a large grassy square, which gave the village a clean appearance. Our poor decrepit mules were let loose in the square and rolled on their backs in the grass trying to ease the pain of the raw exposed flesh. It is a squalid life for man and mule and reminded me of W. C. Fields movie about life on the tundra when he said, "It tain't a fit night out for man nor beast." Only when he said it, it was funny.

We were given a treat for supper, crisp little fried chunks of pork served with rice and gritty bread. Al ate his few pieces of pork voraciously and said it wasn't pork, though we had seen the hanging butchered pig when we came into town.

"I would know if it was pork," he said.

"How?" I asked. "By divine revelation?"

"I would just know. It's different than beef or chicken." So be it. I was beginning to like his religion.

The drovers carry small bags of parched corn and roasted barley meal called *mashka* and mix this with water for their mid-day meal. They didn't offer us any. Just as well, it didn't look appetizing. We only got the scant morning and evening meals. When the mules were unpacked and we could get at our 10-pound tin of cookies, we ate two each.

Tonight we were able to string our hammocks in a shack. Its rough walls had been papered with newspaper but were now covered with dirt that seemed to constantly move. Each village seemed to be filthier, trying to outdo the last. This open air tambo would have been clean if left to nature, but man and beast had rendered it filthy. Al and I slung our hammocks, at least we were off the floor. Jay had the bad luck to be invited to another hovel, the home of a government employee who wanted to talk to a Norte Americano. Jay was our natural leader in South America, taller and more knowledgeable looking. The local priest, a friend of the government official, told us there was a priest in Tena who spoke English.

It was a comfort to climb into our hammocks.

Monday, July 20, Bermejo

"Antonio nearly drove me nuts," Jay said. "He wouldn't shut up. He wants me to get him to America. Just kept on yakking 'till midnight and I had to sleep on his filthy floor. I never want to see this town again. Ever," he said with finality.

"That statement might tempt Loki, the Viking god of mischief, to play tricks," I said, joking. "He likes to test us."

It was a pleasure to leave Baeza after spending the night itching. Our butts and legs were developing sores and ached from the two days of constant riding on wooden saddles. Our stomachs complained from lack of sustenance but the day was clear under a bright sun and the trail looked fairly good.

We got an early start at 8 a.m. and again had to forge several rivers with no bridges, but nothing really dangerous. I was on Seguro (Secure). I liked her. She was aptly named. The beauty of the Andes is difficult to describe – lofty peaks and long ridges of green growth, waterfalls coming out of nowhere, cascading over a thousand feet before hitting the rocks below. But we seldom got a chance to observe these wonders. As I stated before, we mostly saw the rear end of the mule ahead. The trail was so good that Castro put Jay, Al and I in the lead.

About three hours out of Baeza we came to a clearing with a large two-story house, kitchen on the ground off to one side, as usual. Bermejo consisted of two women, one younger and nursing, the other older and pregnant, and eight or nine children who came out to greet *Señor* Castro, "*Hola Pepe, hola Pepe*" and "*Buenos dias, Señor* Castro." We were delighted to dismount and walk around.

The large house at Bermejo, a relic of better times, devoid of furniture. Note kitchen built on ground

Just past the house was the bridge across the Bermejo River that we had to cross. Our first bridge. Evidently the rest, if they had once existed, had washed away or collapsed. We examined it while Castro was greeting the children. It was an 80-foot-long cable suspension bridge with rough boards eight foot long laid across the horizontal cables. The boards were warped and twisted from the weather; none were even. It did not look safe but the drovers had been using it for decades. It must be safe. It doesn't look safe, I thought, but it must be safe.

Jay had a good camera and took pictures throughout the trip. I had borrowed a cheap black and white Brownie and seldom used it. But this bridge looked so rickety that I dug it out of my knapsack and took a picture, just in case it dropped us into the river.

Jay crossing the suspension bridge before it broke

Castro said *hasta la vista*, to his little friends and started for the bridge leading a mule. Castro ordered us across first, one at a time, leading our mules. Jay casually walked across with Adelante. I was next and had a death grip on the cable with my left hand leading Seguro with my right. Al came next with Piqueño while Jay and I watched from the far side. He, too, was casual. One of the little boys came running across with us and waited by the bank. I was relieved to be across safely and we started up the steep trail winding between the trees. We couldn't mount up yet because our animals were followers and wouldn't move unless their nose was pressed to another mule's rear end.

Jay looking at the hole in the bridge from the other side

Half way up this slope we heard a splash. The little boy came up the hill in hysterics, screaming. Then we heard the women screaming, "Pepe! Pepe!" We ran back down to the bridge and saw a gap where planks were missing and Castro standing by the huge rocks in the river 30 feet below, unpacking the mule. His mule had stepped on a bad plank and fell through, wiping out half a dozen planks, dropping both of them in the river. Two other drovers climbed down the bank to help and after some time carried him up into the house. They hauled our supplies, what was left of them, up the steep bank.

We looked for a place recross, but the banks were too steep. No way except the bridge. It took a couple hours for them to get the baggage and mule up the steep bank. Miraculously the mule survived, with only a broken foot and hobbled on three legs, but must have had internal injuries.

They found a few rough boards to spread across the hole in the bridge lengthwise on top of the regular boards. This was dangerous but we had to get back to the other side. Leaving our mules we made our way slowly and cautiously back over the perilous gap, one at a time, with the drovers shouting directions in their dialect of Quechua-Spanish we could not understand. It was every man on his own. I didn't look at Jay or Al but gripped the suspension cable with both hands and hopped my way across. Once across we fell down on the grass exhausted.

Pepe Castro lay on a mat on the dirty house floor with only a thin blanket over him, moaning in pain. The older, pregnant woman was fretting and crying and the drovers sat on the floor on the other side of the room mending their sandals, which they do whenever they have leisure time. Jay asked them in Spanish "Aren't you going to help *Señor* Castro?"

"What can we do? We are only men. We can do nothing. He is in the hands of God. God will decide if he lives or dies." This, in short, is their philosophy of life. We were not under the dominance of the local religion and believed his survival was, at this time, largely up to us. Our first aid book told us Castro was obviously in shock, a dangerous time. I held his head up. He gasped for breath frantically for a minute and then fell limp into my arms. I thought he had died, but was relieved to find he had only passed out. After studying and questioning we decided that he probably had a broken pelvis, a badly sprained or broken ankle, internal bleeding, broken ribs and a broken leg The only medicine we had was aspirin. When he gained consciousness again we got a cup of water and insisted he swallow a couple aspirins. Then wrapped his broken leg in a blanket and tied it securely, following the directions in the manual.

We needed help. Jay's Spanish was good, mine was less and Al could barely say, "*Buenos dias.*" So Jay had to ride back into Baeza, the town he hated, to contact the missionaries in Quito. Garson put the wooden saddle on Enduro and Jay was off, muttering, "It doesn't pay to mess with Loki." He rode the trail alone. I thought one of the drovers would accompany him, but they wouldn't leave their mules. He couldn't get lost, there was only one trail. It soon would be dark. Al and I lit a candle and sat with Castro, trying to comfort him.

The older woman motioned for us to step into the ground floor kitchen a few feet from the house and sat us at a table near the big cast iron stock pot warming over an open fire. I had first choice of three chairs. The one I picked happened to be just under the parrots cage. The bird unerringly dropped kernels of corn into my soup.

The kitchen was the only warm place in the house. Fire is used only for cooking in Ecuador, not warmth, except for the ill. Her son had been kicked by a mule a month earlier and was laid by the fire to recover. He groaned from time to time. If we looked at him, she broke into tears and caterwauled but would immediately stop when we looked away. We stopped looking at him. The smoke from the fire rose and meandered through the grass roof. She fed us *locro* and a small piece of tough, stringy chicken.

A little rice topped off the meal. As we would find out during the next couple days there was always chicken in the pot, but never fully cooked, always tough and stringy because the pot never got hot enough to simmer.

After our meal we asked for soup to take into *Señor* Castro and tried to hold him up and spoon feed him, but to little avail. He was in too much pain to even think of food. We lit a candle by his side and took turns staying with him and sleeping, laying our sleeping bags on the dirty floor. Again, when I was holding him because he had trouble breathing, he gasped, fell back into my arms. Again I thought he had died, but his heart was still beating. A strange sensation, I had never been close to death before. The drovers had gone upstairs to sleep. We forced Pepe to take a couple more aspirins. He was bearing his pain with the *fuerte* (fortitude) of these mountain people.

A bat flew in. Al chased it around swatting at it with a broom, saying he wanted to take it back to Alabama as a souvenir. I was glad he couldn't hit it; it would have stunk badly after a few days. Al was ignorant of the laws of nature and I worried about rabies.

Tuesday, July 21, Bermejo

At about 2 a.m. I heard the dogs barking and stepped out on the landing. It was pitch black. I saw nothing. Out of the darkness I heard someone say in English, "How are you?"

I said "hello" and a hand found mine in the darkness. The voice introduced itself as Padre Mario Canova from Borja. Jay had contacted the missionaries in Quito by radio and they had radioed Padre Canova, who walked eleven kilometers to Baeza and ten kilometers more in the dark to Bermejo. He was a striking man. His blue black beard shone in the candlelight and his eye sparkled.

Everyone got up when they heard his voice. The drovers told him what had happened in Quechua, and we told him what we had done for Castro in English and how Castro had unloaded the mule while standing on one leg after the accident.

The older woman was moaning over Castro like a professional mourner. Al stayed in the corner, he probably had never seen a priest before. The padre was from Italy, spoke seven languages and had been here seven years. After talking to Castro and us he decided it would be better to carry him by stretcher to Baeza and even as far as Quito, if weather would not permit a plane to land.

I was eager to talk to a local who spoke English. I told him how much we admired the fortitude and endurance of the *arrieros*, the drovers, and called them men of steel. I thanked him for coming out in the middle of the night.

"It's why I am here," he said, smiling. He talked to the drovers who asked him many questions. They looked at me and smiled. I waited.

"I told them you thought them '*hombres fortissimo*,' " he said. "They think you are '*medicos*.'"

The old woman, probably the mother of the younger, brought us each a cup of warm *naranja* (orange) juice. The most delicious fruit drink I have ever tasted. He gave Castro an injection of what he called camphor and left us some vials of camphor and a syringe, iodine, cotton and *spermas* (candles). Castro was now able to ask him questions. Padre Canova saw I was curious.

"He wanted to know what the pills were that you gave him. He has never taken a pill. I assured him they were harmless and would ease the pain."

Padre Canova had brought five men with him to make a stretcher and carry *Señor* Castro back to Quito. "They will carry him to Baeza. If weather will not permit a plane to land, they will carry him all the way to Quito."

The padre bid us a cheerful *adios* and was once again off into the black night. The trail, which we had come in on, was dangerous by day but one wrong step at night could be fatal. But this was his territory, his life.

That has to be close to 70 miles, I thought. These truly are *hombres fortissimo*. I knew this man for less than an hour but my admiration for him stays with me to this day, more than 50 years later. To give your life to help those who have not learned to help themselves is commendable. He had dedicated his life to the teachings of Christ and was obviously fulfilled in this task.

My thoughts kept me awake. "Who are the Christians? The overfed Cardinals and Bishops who live in luxury isolated from the destitute and the suffering? The Bible missionaries who persuade the natives to accept Christ and baptize them in the flowing river preparing them for life after death? What about now? Padre Canova is here doing what he can to ease suffering, without glory, honor or official recognition. To bring comfort and cheer, without pride. He fits my understanding of Christ's teaching and is a happy, fulfilled man.

Castro was comforted by the padre's visit and rested peacefully. Al and I alternated shifts, holding Pepe's head up when necessary. I don't know where the five stretcher men slept, I didn't see them again until morning.

The daylight brought a horde of kids to see how their friend was doing. The younger woman was beating a bush with a stick and catching it in a strainer. I watched, curious. She brought it in and held it over the fire, roasting, actually burning, the coffee beans. Then, after mashing then, made us an incredibly delicious cup of coffee. Ah! Fresh beans and river water! Can't be beat. This, with a ladle of *locro* and two chunks of fried dough was breakfast, eaten at the kitchen table, with the parrot dropping corn. I didn't see the drovers eat. I imagine they had their regular parched corn and barley. We were guests and sat on the only chairs in the house. Chickens, dogs and children wandered about the dirt floor at will. Dogs learned to grab fast, growl and eat quickly. The huge soup pot was open. Anything that happens to fall in becomes part of the next meal. I don't know if it ever got emptied or cleaned. I think they just keep adding water, chicken and the odd vegetable. Her son, about 14, lies by the fire, quietly recovering.

The padre's men set to work making a stretcher. One came in to see Castro, who was once again in pain. I broke open a camphor vial while Al sterilized the needle with a match. I fumbled and got air in the ancient syringe on the first try. The padre's man gave me a look of "you gringos can't do anything." He busted the end off a vial with his machete, stuck the needle in, filled it with the camphor, laid it on the dirty floor, put iodine on some cotton, rubbed that on Castro's arm, laid that on the floor, rubbed Castro's arm with his dirty hand, injected the camphor, picked the iodinated cotton off the floor, rubbed it on the arm and smiled at me. I thought, "If Castro survives this he will certainly recover from the fall."

Now Al and I had to decide what to do about paying *Señor* Castro. Do we pay Castro now and trust the other drover to see us through to Tena or do we wait and pay at the end of the line, which was the original agreement? We decided to pay now and trust the drovers to get us to Tena. I gave him 800 *sucres* and wished him well. "*Buena suerte Señor Castro. Vaya con Dios!*" (Good luck. Go with God).

"*Mucho gras, mucho gras,*" he said, squeezing my hand. He indicated *Señor* Garson would be in charge of the mules and us for the rest of the trip.

The padre's men soon had a rough, heavy stretcher made of poles they cut with machetes and laid Castro on it. He was now feeling better from the shot. The older woman brought *naranja* juice for them, which they consumed quickly and went off carrying the stretcher over the mountain on their 70 mile trip to Quito. I did not envy them. The padre inspired everyone to persevere.

Señor Castro being carried 70 miles back to Quito on a makeshift stretcher

The drovers now saw us in a different light. No longer just gringos to be packed over the trail. Garson said "*medicos*" and pointed to his badly scratched legs covered with lesions. As *medicos* we were expected to do something. The first aid kit, a bar of soap, washcloths, towels and a pan of water were all we had. Their legs that were seldom dry below the knees were full of scratches and bruises. To wash and treat these infected and sometimes still bleeding wounds had to hurt. They just smiled. So I said to Al, "Let's see how tough these *hombres* really are." Garson had a large, infected sore on top of an eight-inch scar. I wadded the washcloth and twisted it in the puss filled wound. He didn't flinch. These truly are "*hombres fortissimo.*"

We washed and cleaned the sores and treated them with iodine, which had to sting. No reaction. For the worst wounds we used Vaseline and wrapped them in gauze bandages. They had earned my respect. I felt safe in their hands. Our relationship changed. We had been more of a curiosity, the gringos who provided the day's laughs by falling in the mud or riding around in circles unable to control his mule. Now we became an integral part of the group. But any attempt to communicate was still futile.

Jay returned. He had met Pepe Castro along the trail.

"I asked him how he was doing and he said 'malo, malo,' (bad, bad). I think he will make it. Antonio had the only radio in the area and insisted I spend the night at his hut again. I talked to the missionaries in Quito and they contacted Padre Canova who stopped by on his way here. Interesting man. He had spent seven years in New York.

"Antonio was delighted to see me again and pleaded with me to get the officials in Quito to bring him back to the city. He went on and on. I told him we were going the other way and will not be in Quito. That didn't matter. I got in the sleeping bag and went to sleep. I don't know if he ever shut up. I never want to see Baeza again."

"Don't tempt Loki again," I said.

"Next time you'll go. No matter how bad your Spanish is!" he said. "Also," he continued, "I got terrible diarrhea and had to stop three times along the trail and squat holding the horse's rope. So I took the opium a nurse gave me for that very purpose. It worked. Hope we don't need it again." Jay went on to say he had also contacted Carlos. Lenny had a miraculous recovery and was out on the town. We had suspected as much.

It was time to examine our supplies. Our two lanterns, the cast iron stew pot and camp stove were all broken, plus one coffee cup. We should have gotten tin ones. The gallon can of kerosene was punctured and empty. Our ten-pound tin of biscuits, which we had so carefully rationed out, two each no matter how hungry we felt, hoping it would last the Oriente trip, was smashed and soaked, a pile of wet crumbs. One of the drovers took it for his kids. I thought, "The Southern rebels in the Civil War used to eat their three day supply of side meat as soon as it was distribut-ed. Food keeps better in the belly than in a backpack, was their thinking. Can't be stolen, lost or spoiled. They were right. Not bad advice."

We would have gladly eaten any food left except now it was all gone, one way or another. Even our jar of sugar was broken. We had saved this for quick energy if needed. Our loss made it easier on the pack animals as now there was one less mule.

Two smiling students about 16 years old stopped by for refrescos, (refreshments). Bermejo was a stopping place for trail travelers. They had a cup of *naranja* juice and a slice of cheese and were off down the trail on the way to Archidona, eight miles this side of Tena, and walked the trail to school in Quito a few times each year. What was a miserable journey for us seemed to be just a casual walk for them. They spoke some English and planned to meet us again in Archidona. This trail that was doing us in had been here for 400 years and used regularly by the natives. Were we the only ones suffering? For our proposed trip down the Napo they gave us the same warnings and circled the places on our map along the river where the Aucas lived, adding they were the most dangerous Indians in all of Ecuador, more so than the Jivaros who shrink heads. Then, jokingly, they looked at my head. "They've never had a blond head with a red beard. You might become a trophy." They got a big kick out of the idea. I didn't think it funny

The younger woman was carrying a machete and a live chicken by the feet that had almost no feathers. A chicken for the pot that would never be fully cooked. "Like biting into a ball of string," I said. "Beats just rice and thin soup," Jay said.

We had seen no sign of any man living here. Were the two women and nine children the sole inhabitants?" Who sired the children? Would they learn to read? Where would they go, what would they do? We would carry these questions with us as we continued on.

Bermejo had no outhouse and the river banks were too steep

for easy access. No problem at night, just walk away from the house. But in daylight so many children were milling about it took planning, as the trees were some distance away. I had been constipated for three days and we all needed a bath. When I unzipped my sleeping bag in the morning the stench was over-whelming. Fortunately the sense of smell adjusts quickly. I didn't notice anyone else's odor. We were covered with insect bites that itched and became sores. Now, if I saw a worm, dirt or hair in the food, I just pushed it aside and keep eating.

Our meal that evening was, as anticipated, *locro*, chicken, rice and a bowl of delicious coffee. We had aired our sleeping bags and again laid them on the filthy floor.

Now relaxed I was again besieged by the thought of what I was going to do with the rest of my life. Strange, here in the An-des, about to go through the jungle and I am worried about my destiny. I may not survive this trip. That would certainly solve the problem. I fell asleep with these thoughts buzzing like the *moscos*.

Back on the trail

Wednesday, July 22, Bermejo to Cosanga

We were prepared for an early start. The drovers were packing the mules, eager to get on with it. Our trip was supposed to take five days and this was day six already, with at least two more to go. Jay went to pay the older woman, not knowing if this was our expense or included in the trip price. She told him 120 *sucres*. 120 *sucres*! $7! This was outrageous. Ten scant meals for the three of us and a place to sleep on the dirt covered floor. Were we expected to pay for the drovers as well? She turned on the tears and was caterwauling like a wounded cat. They finally reached an agreement on 60 *sucres* after much haggling. She calmed down and bid us a warm farewell. These women were poor. We didn't begrudge them the money, but we didn't want to get ripped off.

Garson gave me Seguro, bless his heart, and I looked forward to a reasonably manageable day. But one of the mules, Resuelta (yes, the same one that took Al into the mud hole) would not get up. She lay flat on her side and refused to move despite prodding, poking and calls of "*Mulo! Mulo! Levantar! Levantar!*" (Mule! Get up!) Her master *Señor* Pepe Castro was gone and she refused to work for anyone else. I sympathized with her. Her motionless position made the statement "I've had it with this endless, miserable traipsing back and forth, up and down over the Andes. This is the end of my trail, the end of my life. I will not take another step. Here I lie and here I die."

At this point I would have bet everything I had that Resuelta would prevail, that our packs would be divided among the other mules and we would go on without her. I sat back in my wooden saddle, gleefully anticipating an epic struggle between recalcitrant mule and determined drover.

But it was not to be. Garson simply unbuttoned his pants and urinated in the mule's ear. Resuelta jumped up shaking her head vigorously and was saddled and packed in short order. Garson was a pragmatist. But for the chance of birth, he might have become a vice president in a large American corporation.

We dismounted and led our mules across the rough logs placed over the bridge opening that *Señor* Castro had fallen through. Once again I had a death grip on the suspension cable and was ready to let go of Seguro. Again this was every mule for himself. But we made it safely across.

As promised, the trail after Baeza got worse each day. We had to make many detours through rocks and mud and around fallen trees, and shrubbery that tried to rip off our clothes, along with rain. Slow going. Several times we had to dismount and stumble through the soggy ground. Then, after hours of climbing, the trail ended as we came to a wood house at the top of a steep bank that dropped down 50 or 60 feet to the river. We could see a house on the other side of the gorge about 100 feet away. The thought that occurred to each of us was "How the hell are we going to get across this time?" The drovers took the mules and left. Garson stayed with us. The man who lived in the house was looking across the ravine.

To our surprise a man came across the river on a cable we hadn't noticed. He sat on a T-bar suspended from a pulley and pulled hand over hand on the cable, his fingers less than an inch from getting mashed by the pulley. He carried a large bundle wrapped in banana leaves, which we thought must be *chicha*. The cable man and our house man dug into the package and decided to keep it. They placed it under a table covered with a blanket. The cable man went over to the other side and came back with a Quechua Indio straddling him and then went back to collect two more, one at a time. The first Indio looked for the *Chicha* but waited quietly. Then all three searched and asked the house man about the package.

He shrugged his shoulders as though there was no package. One of the Indios lifted the table blanket and found the *Chicha*. He was about to take it when the house man flogged him with a whip. Lash! Lash! Lash! The small Quechua man put his arms up to protect himself and pleaded, to no avail. The house man beat the three of them down the trail. It's a tough life. We did nothing. Not our world. The house man and the cable man were government employees whose job it was to get travelers across the river for free we assumed. It seemed they augmented their income by theft from Indios, the lowest, most vulnerable class.

Jay straddled the cable man to be carried across the ravine. Al went next and then me. It's scary to straddle and hang onto a man looking at the rocks 50 feet below. Real Scary. I had doubts about the whole process but we made it. Such is life in the Andes.

The government employee, the cable man, lived here with his wife and three children. Their house was the first clean house we had encountered in the Andes. Cosanga consisted of three houses, two on the other side of the river and one on this side, with thatched roofs and no chimneys. We had not seen a chimney since we left Tumbaco. Our gentleman host and his smiling gracious wife greeted us warmly. She proudly served us the usual *locro*, chicken and rice with the addition of snowy white potatoes. We smiled and ate. It was tasteless as food is in the Andes but, as always, the coffee was delicious. Our host insisted we sleep in their children's bed, just blankets covering wadding that felt like banana leaves. We protested but it would have been impolite to refuse their hospitality. I have no idea where the children slept.

I again drifted off to sleep thinking of a nice big steak, smothered in onions.

Thursday, July 23, Cosanga

We woke up covered in bug bites. Were they bed bugs? Spiders? *Moscos*? With such a variety of exotic insects flying around, we didn't have a clue.

I couldn't help noticing that Al's Brooks Brothers suit didn't look as spiffy after the mud and rain yesterday. He was still smiling and not complaining. Turning out to be a real adventurer. He'll have some stories to tell his friends in the synagogue back in Birmingham.

After a breakfast of fried dough and delicious coffee, Garson brought the mules up. Jay calculated that we had only traveled eight kilometers yesterday, the most difficult trail so far. Garson indicated we would spend the day climbing up, up, up.

Thankfully it did not rain. As we rose in altitude the grasping bushes grew fewer. The air was pure, the sun was shinning. But our butts were hurting from bouncing up and down in a wooden saddle. We climbed laboriously, up, up, up for several hours before reaching the pass at 16,000 feet. We dismounted and looked out over the 2,000 miles of verdant jungle we were about to plunge into. A breathtaking sight. It took some time for our eyes to adjust to space, after days of staring at the rear of the mule ahead. From our vantage point we could see the jungle stretch out far as the eye could see, finally merging with the horizon in the distance. It seemed impenetrable. Garson let us take our time, we had earned this. If a helicopter had dropped us off we would have taken a casual look and left. But this had taken us eight miserable, wretched, bug bitten, bone jarring days and we drank in this dazzling panorama with delight.

Then back onto Seguro for the descent. It was all downhill from here on. We slid forward in the saddle, less comfortable than going uphill. But not to worry, we'll soon be in Archidona, then Tena. The Province of the Oriente, the Wild Napo Country, is home to the Napos, Zaparos, Jivaros, Quechuas and the recently discovered Aucas. This dense, primeval rain forest has but one trail, the 400-year-old path used by how many thousands before us?

The air was warmer and the growth noticeably different, more tropical. We rode through one area with thousands of fluttering butterflies. Is this where they mate? No time to explore nature. We kept moving. Hunger had been gnawing at us and when the drovers stopped for their *mashka* lunch we greedily ate the last of our can of peanuts, wishing we had more.

We met several Indians on the trail, Quechua, I presume, carrying bundles of *chicha* wrapped in leaves. By late afternoon we came to the village of Jondachi and were given a room on the second floor of a large house, a pleasant change from the tambo huts, but with no beds and no place to hang our hammocks. This felt like the setting of a jungle movie. A Quechua woman in tattered rags and disheveled hair escorted us to a large porch with a table and chairs. What luxury! Surrounded by tropical plants, hanging vines, moss growing over the trees and banana plants, I couldn't help but think of what James Orton wrote a hundred years earlier, "The overpowering beauty of the vegetation soon erased all memory of the squalor and lifelessness of the previous days."

Alas, not all had changed. Our Quechua hostess spread out a grubby, stained tablecloth. This ritual was left over from some more gracious time but the civilized details have been forgotten. Supper brought serendipity. Good *locro* soup, if somewhat sandy, potatoes, chicken, fried dough, yucca sticks and coffee. Our appetites were eased but not sated. We complimented our hostess. She smiled graciously. The six inch moth that flew into Jay's coffee did not perturb us. Jay, as I would have done, simply picked it out and kept drinking. We were becoming acclimated and starting to relax, though our bodies were full of bites and ached from the mule ride. Al seemed fine, a small man still in his teens, thrilled by it all, comfortable in his Brooks Brothers suit, which was now showing some serious signs of wear. Oh well, it's probably guaranteed.

Garson stopped by to tell us (in Spanish dialect) that a bus at Archidona, 33 kilometers down the trail, would take us the last ten kilometers into Tena. Jay questioned him, "A bus? In the jungle?"

"*Si, Señor. Una buseta.*"

Jay announced that once in Archidona he would never get on

the back of a mule again. I advised caution. The Viking gods make sport of grandiose pronouncements, but what did I know?

With darkness came the enthralling cacophony of the jungle engulfing us in dozens of different calls and chattering, endless communication between birds and animals we could not see. On it went. Who were they talking to? What were they saying? And why? We would never know. This was not our world, not our language. Elated to finally be in the jungle, Jay and I lingered over coffee and cigarettes, which fitted well into this wild environment. Al didn't smoke or drink coffee. His loss. The surrounding racket was friendly, soothing and relaxing, not scary like a Tarzan movie.

Things were better, we thought as we crawled into our sleeping bags on the hard floor, and would continue to get better. Perhaps our bites would heal. We asked no one in particular, "Don't the natives get bitten? We never see them scratch," and, "What do these millions of bugs eat when we're not here."

Friday, July 24, Jondachi

Next morning, after a bowl of coffee and two chunks of fried dough we mounted up for our last day on the mules, eager to get to Archidona and the bus. It was an easy downhill trail. About noon we came to a *hacienda* with a porch loaded with fruit, some of it spoiling. We dismounted and asked the Spanish gentleman if we could buy some fruit.

"*No se puede*" (That is not possible), he said, politely. Why, we thought? It is laying here rotting. Jay tried again, "*Por favor, Señor*, we would like to buy some of your fruit."

Once again he politely turned down our offer, but then went on to say, smiling, in Spanish, "Please help yourselves to all you want," waving his hand over the piles of fruit.

We thanked him and plunged in, gorging ourselves on *naranjas*, bananas, large sweet grapefruit we could not get our hands around, a small fruit that tasted like apricot, oranges and

other delicious fruits we had never seen before. We stuffed ourselves but found that fruit alone does not sate hunger, just makes
you full. With aching stomachs we thanked him profusely and
climbed back on our mules.

The other animals were out of sight, a half hour ahead of us.
Jay went on with Adelante but I dropped my shirt, which I had
taken off and tied around my waist. Al, behind me, got off his
mule to pick it up. When he tried to get back on Piqueño bucked
him off. I tied Seguro to a vine and held Piqueño while Al got
back on. Now Jay was out of sight. Once I was back in the saddle Seguro panicked at not seeing the rear end of another mule
walking in front of her and ran frantically. I was on a runaway
mule, doing the best she could with her stiff-legged gallop. It is
not difficult to stay on a runaway mule; they mostly just bounce
up and down. I took off my shirt and held it over Seguro's head,
having read somewhere that a runaway horse will stop when
they can't see. Seguro did stop but threw her head up, hitting
my head, nearly knocking me out in the process. I kept my arms
around her neck, trying to keep from passing out while she bel-
lowed the most god awful braying – heehaw, heehaw, heehaw.
Isolated from her fellows she couldn't handle being alone. Al
caught up with us and I motioned for him to go around. I took
my shirt off Seguro's head and once she saw Piqueño's tail she fell
into step. I was learning more about mules than I ever wanted to
know. I hoped I would never ride one again, but didn't express
my thoughts aloud. Loki just might be listening.

This was our longest day's ride, 35 kilometers to Archidona.
The caravan was there, mules grazing on the green grass, our
arrieros, (drovers), eating their *mashka*. We lay down on the soft
grass, happy to be off these dreadful beasts once and for all. The
sky was blue; the air clean and pure, life was good. The students
found us and gave us a delicious fruit drink. Ecuadorians are
personable and hospitable.

Jay with students we met in Bermejo

Then Garson came over and indicated for us to mount up again. "What a sense of humor," I thought. "He knows we've had it with mules."

"*No mas mulo*," I said, laughing. "*Vamous buseta*."

"*No Buseta*," he said, pointing at the bus some distance away. Then we saw the bus engine lying off to one side on the ground.

"*No buseta*," I said, stupidly translating the obvious for Jay and Al. It's eight more kilometers to Tena. We would have to get back on these stinking, noxious, foul-tempered beasts. Jay didn't say a word, just walked off leading his mule. Al did the same. Not me, damn it. I paid for this ride and I'm going to ride. I mounted Seguro and dug my heels into her flanks. She refused to move. Again, she refused to move. I yelled, "Listen, you stupid mule, I'm in charge here, and I'm going to ride." No response.

I dismounted to find a switch and had no more than hit the ground when Seguro took off to catch up with the walkers. She, too, had enough. "The hell with it," I thought, "it's not worth it." I, too, walked.

Or rather, trudged. Aching and sore from the wooden saddles and stiff legged jouncing, walking on a rough trail was not much better, but at this point it was not my choice. I did not have to lead Seguro, she followed the tail ahead of her. The trail, full of rocks and overgrowth, after three hours led us at last to a ramshackle, unpainted two story building made of rough cut lumber which boldly stated, HOTEL TENA, in large letters. What delight! A hotel! Beds, mattress, sheets, closets with clothes hangers, pillows, showers. Ah.

Garson unpacked the mules and we carried our duffles up the stone steps into the lobby. "We would like rooms for the night," Jay said in his best Castiliano to the rather disheveled owner sitting at his table. It was done. We were here. The mule trip was over. For the modest price of 17 *sucres* each (a dollar and a quarter American, which we soon realized was a rip-off, even with meals included) we were shown to our rooms.

Each room was dirty, damp and cold, without window or fire, not even a wash basin. But there was a light bulb hanging down from the ceiling, which worked when the village generator started at seven p.m. The too short beds (at least there were beds) consisted of a frame with slats running crosswise covered with a thin mattress. Jay and I were both jarred back into the reality of where we were and met in the hall, laughing. Al, however, was still caught up in the illusion of being in a hotel. He showed up a few minutes later in his robe, with a towel draped over his arm, soap and washcloth in hand and asked the hotel owner, "Which way to the bathroom?" The owner did not speak English and we did not know the Spanish work for toilet. I couldn't resist. "Downstairs, straight out the back door fifteen steps, then turn right." He left smiling, anticipating a nice warm shower, I'm sure. He had all the appurtenances, which we didn't.

He returned frowning. "There's nothing but jungle back there."

"Yep, that's the place, the main bathroom, to accommodate all and sundry. Welcome to the jungle." I couldn't help but notice that Al's robe and towel had suds on them. I didn't have to ask. Al volunteered, "My can of shaving lotion exploded coming over the Andes."

We found out the next day that there was one outhouse in Tena on a trail some distance from the hotel, a seldom used small grass roofed Tambo with a hole in the floor. It must have been erected for the two government officials from Quito.

We didn't wash, the river was some distance away and it was already dark. The evening meal was standard fare and we were glad to get to our beds. Problem was the sideboards spread and the slats fell out. We weighed more than the natives. Al was okay but jay and I had to put our duffles under the slats. Still it beat sleeping on the floor.

~ Part Two: Arrive ~

Saturday, July 25, Tena

We checked in at the police station, which took some time. Officials are never in a hurry. They have little to do and like to exercise their importance. The head man (police chief? Army officer? Government official?) was puzzled that Jay and I had tourist cards and Al had a visa. I'll spare you the details but it went on and on. They had probably not seen a tourist card before. At one point Jay nudged me and almost burst out laughing. He was studiously examining Jay's passport, upside down. Finally they decided our papers were okay but we needed a military permit. A military permit? In the middle of the jungle? With no military this side of the Peruvian border? So much government for so few people. It cost us each seven *sucres*, which meant the police would eat better tonight, at least the head man. Neither they nor the hotel owner had heard anything about Lenny.

Tena Hotel keeper with his five daughters

We went to see the English speaking priest, father Teodoro Rosero, to radio father Mario Canova and find out if *Señor* Castro got home alive. He told us to come back at 7:30 *mañana*.

To assuage my conscience, after a good night's rest and realizing I would never see Seguro again, I had saved one of my two small chunks of fried dough from breakfast and found the grazing mules. I held the treat out to Seguro who laid her ears flat against her head as she reached for it, the most emotion I ever saw her display. Once that was gone she went back to grazing, ears at ease. I tried to scratch her head and pat her neck but she wasn't interested.

"Look, you stupid mule," I said, "I just gave you half my breakfast. The least you could do is acknowledge my existence. You kept me from being washed away in the flood or being carried off the side of the mountain in the landslide. You didn't dump me in a mud-hole or brush me off on a tree branch or step on a bad board and plunge us through the bridge to the rocks below. I am grateful for that."

She didn't raise her head. All she wanted to do was graze. I was just another load of baggage on one of her endless trips across the Andes. She had done her job and now it was over. Jay, Al and I would spend the next four weeks in a dugout canoe going through the jungle on the Napo River. She will go back and forth over the Andes again and again until she dies on the trail. As I left the paddock I looked back one last time, hoping to make final eye contact. We would never meet again. But she did not look up. I said "*Muchas Gratias, Seguro. Adios.*"

The mule trip was over, never to be forgotten. For Jay and I, it was indeed "the nine most wretched, miserable, wet, cold, hungry, bone-jarring, bug-bitten days of our lives." For teen age Al it was his first, and probably only adventure. He would tell the story whenever he had the chance, for the rest of his life. I could imagine him as an old man, relating it to his grandchildren.

But for Pepe Castro, Garson and the other *arrieros* it was just another trip, their way of life. We found *Señor* Garson and the rest, thanked them *muchas gratias*, bid them *adios* and wished them well. I admire and respect, but do not envy them. They truly are *hombres fortissimo*.

The four of us on the steps of the Tena Hotel.
Top to bottom: Jack, Jay, Al, Lenny

Part Three:
Through the Jungle to the Amazon
by Dugout Canoe

~~~

~ Plan ~

~~~

Sunday, July 26, 1959 - Tena

Tena is a large town for the Oriente. More than two hundred inhabitants are spread out over a cleared area surrounded by jungle. It's the last stopping point between the Andes and the jungle rivers. Not even grass grows in the streets, a busy village. The natives, for the most part, live in mud hovels, without windows, tenanted by vermin and ragged poverty. They live for the day, accept life as it is and don't plan for some distant future.

Father Teodoro Rosero had learned by radio that Pepe Castro survived the trip and was at his home in Tumbaco. Good news but we wondered if he would ever run mules again. I stayed, happy to speak English with the priest, while Jay went a mile across the creek to Dos Rios to meet the Conns, a missionary family. Father Rosero showed me the Catholic church, a modest building, and proudly pointed out two silver candle sticks. I thought to myself, "Why don't they sell the silver and feed the poor?" Later, I realized that the candles were a delight to the eye, a permanent joy that gave light to the darkness of the world. Food would be gone and forgotten in a day or two.

His room in the small monastery had one window and was furnished with a desk, stool and a cot. A collection of two dozen huge insects, some more than six inches long, was pinned to the adobe wall. Impressed, I said, "You have a wonderful collection. How long did it take you to gather them?"

Puzzled, he said, "They fly in my window." I examined huge moths, large bellied, odd shaped bugs and other strange creatures.

"If this one bites you, you die," he said, pointing at a large proboscis on one. "These you can eat, if you run out of food," he added, denoting a large bug that looked fat and juicy, but not tasty. And so on.

"Would you like to have them?"

I couldn't believe my ears. He would part with them? Well, more flew in daily. We packed them in a small case and I danced back to the hotel. It hadn't crossed my mind why I wanted them or what I would do with them. But they now were mine and would go with me home to Minnesota.

Jay returned with the Conn's two sons and Lenny, who smiled and said, "I have been sick, throwing up since the day you left. But after a week I somehow managed, with terrible diarrhea, to catch a bus to Baños and from there caught a missionary plane to Shell Mera. They gave me a horse and said 'Just sit, he knows where to go'. So I rode twenty miles through the jungle. Not the same as a mule but here I am. I moved in with the Conn family and now I'm feeling fine."

The whole story had an aura of mendacity about it. He said nothing about his miraculous cures from malaria and hepatitis. We didn't ask. If only the long nosed affliction of Pinocchio applied to humans!

Shell Mera was an exploration site for the Dutch Oil Company. They had to abandon it in 1948 because the Aucas were killing employees. It now belongs to the Mission Aviation Fellowship that uses it as their main base of operations. It was kind of them to fly Lenny in and give him a horse, but not surprising. They are Christians. Lenny is a con man.

The trip to the Conns' home was about a mile. We rented three mules for our luggage. I wondered, as always, "Do we really need all this baggage?" Fact is we didn't know what we may or may not need and were afraid to toss anything. As we approached the Tena River a smiling man came out of a hovel, beckoned us to sit in his dugout canoe, poled us across and asked no payment. This is where he lived and this was his job. I never discovered who paid these various people who perform small services at no charge.

The Conns, in their mid-thirties, welcomed us warmly and gave us their two upstairs bedrooms with double beds and real springs. I wanted to jump up and test the springs but restrained myself. Ah, how good to be among giving, fundamentalist Christians who give and ask nothing in return. They knew and had contact with some of the missionaries my home church in Minnesota was supporting.

Each room had a wash basin and a pitcher of water. We were back in civilization so we washed up. Mrs. Conn gave us some of Mr. Conn's clothes and the local washer women would beat our dirty clothes on the rocks in the river. I couldn't help wondering if Al's Brooks Brothers wool suit would survive this beating.

Supper was a delight, Swedish meatballs and mashed potatoes with gravy, a real Minnesota meal, the most memorable meal of the trip. We later found out that it was their week's allotment of meat from Quito and they had to procure more locally. They didn't stint for guests.

The Conns did not smoke or drink. After supper I asked Mr. Conn if I might smoke. After stammering, he said, "Just not on Sunday when the church attendees are here." We smoked outside, far from the house and church.

Lenny had gone into Napo before we arrived and arranged for a canoe and paddlers. We needed a larger dugout so the Padrone sent two of his natives up river to procure one. The 30th of July was our day of departure so we enjoyed a few days of pleasant relaxation.

Monday – Thursday, July 27 — 31, 1959 - Dos Rios

We were eager to get into the jungle and took the necessary precautions, loose pants to protect from snake bites, heavy boots, rifles, pith helmets. Proceeding cautiously along the trail, careful of each step, searching the trees overhead for hanging snakes, listening for jaguar or peccary crashing through the underbrush, thinking of the dangers recounted in Rivers Ran East, we trod deeply into the thick, dark growth surrounding us. It was quiet, calm and peaceful, but we stayed alert. Soon we relaxed a little and then, hearing a noise behind us, whirled around with rifles poised and stood there, dumbfounded. The Conns' nine year old boy, Billy and a native boy were running barefoot down the path and playing. We smiled sheepishly. Billy told us that there were few animals along this trail, which had been hunted a good deal. And, if there were any, our noisy clomping would scare them off. As for snakes, it's rare to see twenty footers like those hanging out of trees in the movies. We shouldered our rifles. Except for the birds and an occasional small monkey peeking out from behind a treetop leaf to see the "great white hunters," the jungle was quiet and peaceful.

We were a curiosity. The boys from the village called us cowboys. Where did they hear that term? One handed me a lasso. I swung it a couple times and luckily roped one of them. Then another farther away. I was as surprised as they were. They yelled "*Vaquero! Vaquero!*" (Cowboy) then something about a caballo. Two of them ran off and came back with a horse. I climbed into the saddle to show I knew how to handle a horse. After a few laps around the paddock at different gates, my caballo galloped, straight for the river and did not respond to the reins. The boys were laughing and running behind. I was no longer in control so I clasped my hand on the saddle horn, pushed my feet forward in the stirrups and sat back. El caballo stopped dead just at the brink of the river. I managed to stay on but both my legs ended up around the horse's neck.

The boys were disappointed. This horse had been trained to toss unsuspecting riders into the river.

The natives used what was available to survive. In the rain they placed the stem of a huge leaf in their waist band that hung forward over their head and kept them dry. At night they caught dozens of fireflies and put them in a jar to light the trail. These fireflies have two white lights in front and one blinking red tail light. The jar held at knee level glows sufficiently to see the trail.

We gorged ourselves at every meal. Mrs. Conn was more aware of the tough trip ahead than we were. My stomach wasn't used to this and I suffered indigestion. It was five days of feasting and resting with a kind family of four well-mannered children and a monkey, Herbie, tied in a tree. I tried to make friends with Herbie, but he would have none of it, and chomping his cute little white teeth into me several times. The Conn's thought it might be my red beard, which was by now full.

We swam and washed in the river and daily a cute girl aged 15 or 16 displayed herself on the other bank in her green swimsuit. Maybe she wanted to go to America with the gringos. We remembered the admonition: "When the females start looking good, it's time to get out of the jungle." She didn't look that good.

A young boy with an eight foot blowgun wanted me to bring my 22 caliber pistol and go hunting with him, but something else was always going on when he showed up. Blowguns are very accurate for 60 feet or more. The user slices a six-to-ten-inch dart off a thin hardwood slab secured to his waist. He wraps it with down and dips the tip in curare poison, which paralyzes the animal, usually small game. Holding it to his mouth, he aims and blows a quick burst of air that propels the dart to it's objective. He gave me a demonstration. I wish I had learned to use it.

Al and Lenny quickly bonded and went off together comparing notes on psychology. The third day a missionary couple who had lived with the Jivaros for 30 years stopped by en route to Quito. 30 Years! Imagine, spending that much of your life with headhunters. They believed it is up to them to get the word out before it is too late to save the heathen from the lake of fire and brimstone and are willing to risk their own lives for this belief.

The missionary was an interesting man. I never did know his name, we only saw him that one day, but Jay and I talked to him at length.

"We have been fortunate," he said. "They have accepted us. The Jivaro have never been conquered despite fighting that goes back several hundred years. The Spanish just gave up on them and left them alone. Some tribes live peacefully and trade with the outside world, but there are many tribes that still go on raids for young wives. Our tribe is now monogamous and wears clothing. Some tribes still sell shrunken heads for which there is a ready world market. But now they mostly shrink monkey heads to sell. The wilder tribes only shrink a head if they believe that person has harmed them, or if someone has the bad luck to be there during an illness, he is believed to be the cause."

"Do they accept visitors?" I asked.

"Should you meet them they have an elaborate ritual. It can take a half hour for them to say "good morning". First they remove the bone stuck through the skin just under the lower lip and spit at your feet. Then you must spit at their feet. They have the spitting advantage through the hole under their bottom lip, but you do the best you can. They spit at your feet again. Your *arriero*,(guide and paddler) will know what to do. They will say "we greet you" in Jivaro to which he will reply "we greet you". After repeating this several times, the Jivaro might say, "You are with white men" to which your *arriero* will say "We are with white men". This also will be repeated several times. Next the Jivaro will say "The white men have come a long way". Be prepared for this to go on and on. They will not be hurried. Finally, when they have found out all they want to know, they will take you through a lengthy farewell and you can be on your way. That is, if you have not offended them."

While we were talking, the daily rain fell and we ducked under the trees. A rainbow appeared. He continued, "They believe if you can get to the base of the rainbow the evil spirits cannot harm you. No pot of gold for them."

I asked him about the Aucas. "Auca is a Quechua word meaning wild people. They may be an offshoot of the Zaparo tribe. They are also called Sabela and Aushiris. When the natives along the Napo River speak of Aucas they are referring to two or possibly three tribes, who are constantly at war with each other. Little was known about them until a few years ago because of their practice of killing everyone who saw them. These naked savages, who paint their bodies, inhabit the area between the Curaray and Napo rivers, never crossing either. Intertribal warfare has cut their numbers drastically. It's amazing any are left.

"The villagers fear them. They wait in the underbrush for days to capture a young girl. Seeing a suitable victim, they dart out, throw her over their shoulder and disappear into the jungle. Or they kill people without reason, reportedly throwing babies up in the air and catching them on spears.

"Rachael Saint is hoping to bring them to Christ. She learned their language from an Auca girl called Dayuma, whom the Aucas had tried, but failed, to kill. Rachel's husband, Nate, and four others flew over the Aucas for months, dropping presents and shouting over the plane's loudspeaker, "We are your friends. We want to help you". When they felt the time was right they landed. The Aucas sent them a nubile young girl, whom they called Delilah and rejected, considering her evil, believing her to be a temptation from the devil. And, as you know, they were all speared."

I couldn't help thinking that the Aucas had allowed themselves to be seen and sent the missionaries the best gift they had to offer, a young girl. The Aucas live nude and have no Christian concept of sin. Rejecting her was an insult. The missionaries didn't have to think of her as a sex object, just a gift. Maybe if they had sent her back with a smile and an arm full of gifts they would still be alive.

If a spacecraft flew over me with someone shouting, "We are your friends. We want to help you," I, too, would be disconcerted and try to avoid them.

"Rachael Saint," he continued, "managed to move in with the Auca tribe and live with them. This brave soul says they let her stay because they thought she was looking for a husband and was no threat. She is succeeding, God bless her."

Jay had talked to Rachael in Quito between her visits to the Aucas. One of the Aucas, George, who had talked to the missionaries, was subsequently buried alive, at his own request. The Aucas believe in transmigration. That is, when a man dies he is reborn as an animal and a woman as a bird. Those buried alive have the edge over those buried dead in the next life. One day as Mrs. Saint was sitting by the river, George's wives (he had three) playfully kicked sand around her. When she began to squirm, they laughed and said, "That's the way George squirmed when we buried him."

The subject of Aucas came up again after supper. Six months earlier they had killed a Canadian. He wanted to meet the natives and went alone into the jungle to seek them. After a few days in their territory, they let him see them. He panicked and fired his rifle at them. They speared him. It was not Rachael's tribe but she heard about it, saying, "The natives know your presence long before you know theirs. It's best to be just passing through. If they are accepting guests, they will make it known, if not, they will also make it known."

Again we were admonished not to land on the right bank of the Napo River in Auca territory.

This talk made me apprehensive. Jay was not, he would deal

calmly with whatever happened. Al and Lenny were mentally still in the safety of the civilized world. In the Andes, three days from the nearest small village, Al had looked up from his mule at a small clearing, a steep grassy slope, and said, "This would be a nice place for a summer home." How to get materials in, who would build it, what could you do there and why you would want to be there, never entered his mind. His mind was still in Alabama, thinking of wealth and property. Lenny, on the other hand, was so impervious that nothing frightened him, and we were about to penetrate the jungle together. Thank God for Jay.

Jay tested the rivers for minerals with positive results, but it would take a lot of time and money to follow the rivers and to find the origin of the minerals. This we could not do. At least he had provided the reason for the trip. Al finally managed to bag a vampire bat with a broom and packed it in salt to become part of our memorabilia. I had my doubts, but what did I know? In the evenings we played Peggity, a children's game, with the Conn family, which fit nicely into the quiet life.

Friday, July 31, 1959 - Dos Rios
    Hearing nothing about the canoe, I went into Tena with Billy, Conn's youngest son, and found that it is in Napo ready to leave, *mañana* at 5 a.m. Again we forgot that *mañana* means sometime after today, but not necessarily tomorrow, and that we had chartered the canoe and it would not leave without us.

We rented three mules for our luggage and four horses to ride for 76 *sucres* ($5.70), packed our duffles and thanked the Conns for their wonderful hospitality, knowing we would never see them again. These kind people gave us hard boiled eggs, bread and a large tin of peanuts.

It was after 6 p.m. and dark by the time we set off, traipsing over a rough, rocky trail with mud-holes and narrow foot bridges. We had thought of walking, but Jay didn't object to riding a horse. My foot was still numb from the mule trip and once in the wooden saddle my rear hurt, but otherwise things were well. The mules knew the trail pitfalls that we could not see but our boy *arriero* kept beating the last horse. We finally told him to let the beasts set their own pace.

At last we were in the jungle. My mind started to adjust to our new world. We saw little, but felt the trees and vines crowding in from both sides of the narrow trail and over our heads. Do snakes crawl at night? Or hang out of trees waiting to drop on prey? Do Jaguars kill and eat horses? Will tapirs charge? Are they dangerous? I had trusted the animal I straddled, as he seemed to know what he was about.

We accomplished the eight kilometers in a little over two hours, were happy to find the village of Napo was larger than expected and had an electric generator running from 7 pm until 10 pm. We tipped our boy *arriero* five *sucres* and checked into the local rough board hotel, with bed slats that fell out. The manager informed us that we were not leaving *mañana* but *mañana passado*, (the day after tomorrow). I wouldn't bet on it.

Saturday, August 1, 1959 - Puerto Napo

Breakfast consisted of *tortillas*, whey and delicious *café con leche*. News had preceded us. One of the locals hopefully informed Jay that there was gold in the Napo River, but Jay is no longer testing. He is trying to sell his gun, but to no avail. I bought a small jaguar skin. Al found some clothes for sale and either packed or trashed his Brooks Brothers suit. A man stopped by to show us his Auca spear. Lenny wanted it.

"*Compro. Quantos Questa?*" (I will buy, how much are you asking?)

"*No se vende,*" (Not for sale) he answered. We had heard that the Aucas only leave spears in someone they've killed. It was a beautifully carved shaft of shiny black wood, eight feet long, triangularly sided with barbs on the pointed end. Lenny thought everything was for sale and offered him twenty American dollars, a large sum. The señor was offended and said that this spear had killed his father; he would never sell it. *"No se puede vende. Adios,"* and he was gone. Lenny shrugged his shoulders.

"I don't understand these people. He could feed his family for two months with that much money."

Juan, a young man who spoke English, told us the river is dangerous from here to Coca. *"Muy pelegro,"* he said, reverting to Spanish, and spoke of all the canoes that had been sucked into whirlpools and eddies, losing luggage and sometimes passengers. "My brother almost went to the bottom in his canoe."

"He was a poor paddler," a man behind us mumbled in Spanish. Juan went on to say the Aucas area is 50 kilometers down river, between the Napo and Jaguar Rivers. "You must stay away from the right bank. They will kill you," he said thrusting his thumb into his breast. Juan stayed with us.

The dugout canoe was pulled up on the rocky shore and fitted out for the trip down river. The Napo is narrow here, less than a hundred feet across. Our dugout canoe is just over 30 feet long and three and a half feet wide in the center. It had been burned and chopped out with an adz, then the shell was shaped from stem to stern. The two-foot deep gunnels, three to four inches thick, looked strong enough to survive the rapids.

The Padrone was giving orders to a dozen indios. Juan enlightened us.

"He is in control of everything, having had several wives and mistresses and access to the young girls as they come of age. He has populated most of Napo himself. These Quechua Indios are his property. They are not slaves but can't leave. "You must pay me for all the years I have fed you and given you shelter."

"How much?" they ask and he gives an amount. If they somehow manage to come up with the money, their bill has strangely

gone up and they still can't go. As they can neither read nor write
there is little they can do. These peaceful people are easy to swin-
dle. They have neither the identity of tribal life nor the support of
civilization. Your paddlers belong to him, will do as they are told
and they will not try to escape."

He talked about the Aucas and claimed not only to have met,
but also forewarned, the Canadian they speared.

We examined the dugout and wondered if it had room for
four paddlers, their supplies and us. Once the boards for seats
and luggage were set, we paid the Padrone 320 *sucres* and
watched as he gave each Quechua paddler 20 *sucres* ($1.50). All
were barefoot. One had enormous feet with toes that shot out in
all directions, never having worn shoes. The lead paddler, Jose,
spoke some Spanish. Juan was not finished admonishing us, "Do
not piss in the river," he said.

"Okay. We'll have the paddlers keep an eye out for a nice rest
stop where they have clean toilets," Lenny replied sarcastically.

Juan looked puzzled for a minute, and then realized he was
being kidded.

"I am serious. If you are standing even in knee water, a little
fish, less that an inch long (he indicated with his thumb and fore-
finger) can swim up your *piroca* and lodge there." He paused to
let this sink in. Then, "You cannot piss him out. His barbs are too
strong. Then your belly swells up with piss and after two or three
days you must cut your *piroca* off or die," he said. "*Mio amigo*
(My friend) had to." He held his hand by his groin and made a
slashing move with the other hand. He was not joking.

Of all the ways the jungle can harm or kill you, this seemed the
worst. We started back to the hotel with some apprehension. An
old man who lived in an adobe shanty invited us in for fruit and
coffee. He, Manuel Rivadeneira, was 78 years old and had lived in
Puerto Napo all his life. He spoke to us of heroes of the past.

"Four hundred years ago Orellano set out from here to travel the length of the Amazon to the Pacific Ocean. He and his men suffered greatly. Many died from poison darts and spears, many more from hunger and jungle diseases. Orellano himself died of illness and heartbreak after losing so many of his crew. Eight million natives lived in the Amazon basin at that time."

He looked up to see our reaction. We were impressed by his knowledge.

"Now we are only 200,000 from here to the Pacific, thanks to European diseases." Another pause. "At the confluence with the Amazon, Orellano was attacked by a tribe of fair-skinned women who fought fiercely. He called them Amazonas after the Greek legend and that is how the mighty river got its name. After managing to fend them off and escape, some of his men wanted to capture them for wives, but Orellano said, 'No.' They would never be submissive enough to be of benefit. And they might kill you. Why are there no men with them now?'"

Manuel talked of other things, including the Aucas, about which we had heard enough. We asked him about the little fish that swim up your *piroca*. He affirmed this. "You must be careful," he consoled. "Better to lose a hand or foot than something that important." He smiled. He also assured us of the abundance of food in the *selva* (jungle), tapirs (a large pig-like animal with a long snout), peccary (a smaller pig-like animal), *monos* (monkeys) and birds of all kinds. An abundance of food sounded good so we bid buenos noches.

This night, the eve of my 25th birthday and the beginning of our trek into the jungle, we broke out the carefully preserved for a special occasion, a small bottle of apricot brandy and each had a snort.

"Here's to the *selva*," I said, "May we claim it and not the other way around."

"I'm not afraid," Lenny said a bit arrogantly.

"Nor I," agreed Al. Jay nodded. Fear was not to be shared or experienced although this was supposedly the most dangerous part of our journey. I did not mention that we had food for only four meals, hoping Manuel Rivadeneira was right, that the jungle was bountiful.

The town generator shut down at 10 p.m. We crawled into our sleeping bags on the bed slats that fell out, listening to the jungle noises. Out of the blackness came beautiful singing, three or four men with guitars serenading some lucky *señorita*, we thought. No. They were outside our windows. As is the custom, we were the guests and these kind, gracious people sent us off with best wishes. It reminded us of the warmth and unselfishness the Ecuadorians had shown us. We could not help but love them. But as I lay there my old nemesis returned. What would I do with the rest of my life? I can't stay in the *selva* forever and would soon have to face the music. But not tonight! Tonight I can put all that off, relax and sleep.

~~~
## ~ Part Three: Travel ~
~~~

Sunday, August 2, 1959 - Puerto Napo, Ecuador

Mañana arrived. The shouting of the paddlers awakened us as they came to gather our bags. We dressed, packed, had a quick *desayuno* of fried dough and *café con leche* and set off for the canoe. The street was lined with people, half the town had come to see the gringos off. I took a quick picture of our hotel owner, Shimora and his *niñas* and promised to send him one. But, like so many promises, I forgot. I recently found his address in my notes, more than 50 years later.

Four paddlers, a 10 year old boy and another man were in the canoe. One paddler sat at the bow point, three just behind him, then the boy, our luggage, our place to sit and more luggage. Jose was behind us at the helm, the extra man next to him. Manuel Rivadeneira had arrived before us and was rapping his cane on the side of the canoe, shouting at the paddlers in Quechua.

I asked Juan, "What is he telling them and why? They don't belong to him."

"There are two classes of people, Blanco and Negro, white and black. We are Blanco, the Indios are Negro. He is a Blanco and is telling them, in no uncertain terms to be careful with you, don't lose the bags and don't tip the canoe over, or else."

"How do you know who is Blanco and who is Negro?" I held my white arm next to his tan arm.

"It is obvious at a glance and has nothing to do with skin color. You have a wrist watch. I can read and write. *Señor* Manuel Rivadeneira is in authority. Everyone knows what they are."

I let it go and asked "Manuel ended his orders to the Indios with 'or else.' Or else what?"

"I don't know Quechua well, but it sounds serious," he said with a smile. Manuel continued giving them hell, like they were already guilty of something. They were huddled together and promised to do what he demanded.

Our dugout canoe with four paddlers and a younger brother. Jose far right

Loading, Padrone, just ahead of Lenny, giving final orders

Down the Napo river to the Amazon by Dugout Canoe

We thanked the hotel keeper, Manuel, Juan and anyone else within ear shot and climbed in. As we shoved off and caught the current, Juan shouted his last admonition, "Don't piss in the river." Lenny stood up, put his hand by his groin like he was holding his *piroca* and made a slashing motion with his other hand. "It'll be all right," he shouted, "It's too long now." Maybe Lenny would be okay. He did have a sense of humor.

The river quickly widened to 100 yards, the current increased from six knots to 15 or 20, we guessed. The dexterity of the paddlers was put to the test in the first 20 minutes. The bowman signaled right or left with his raised paddle to Jose at the helm. We went around swirling whirlpools and eddies, avoiding getting sucked in. Then all four paddlers stood up, shouting in Quechua, and pointing with their paddles. Jose guided us to the left bank and motioned for us to get out and walk downstream as they circumvented dangerous eddies and turbulent waters.

It was pleasant walking on the narrow, rocky beach next to the 80-foot impenetrable solid wall of jungle. On one of these drop offs, I got interested in the pools left by the shifting river. Were there fish left in any of them? Edible fish? The others had wandered on ahead. Caught up in the moment, I didn't look where I was going and stepped in quicksand. Immediately in up to my knees, I instinctively fell backwards and rolled out. The others were around a bend and would not have heard my shouting over the roar of the rapids. I resolved to be more watchful and careful.

Paddlers taking canoe through rapids after putting us ashore

On these diversions Jay and I were engrossed in the river and jungle. Al and Lenny walked on in front, deep in conversation. I assumed it was about Freud or Jung. Then, after the rapids, they sat in the front of the dugout, just behind the paddlers. Al asked to borrow my 22 caliber pistol. He had never seen a gun up close, and enjoyed shooting at birds in the trees, although there weren't many. He shot a lot, trying to aim. We were safely past the rapids when Jose pulled the canoe to the left bank. "*Lluvia*," (rain) he said. "*Lluvia*," pointing to the sky. We looked up. Not a cloud in sight. He made motions for us to cover ourselves so we dug out our ponchos, not a moment too soon. The paddlers covered the canoe and themselves with huge leafs. Then a 15 minute deluge hit us.

We praised Jose in Spanish (of which he spoke little and the paddlers none) for getting us safely through the rapids. He translated for them. They beamed and smiled proudly.

Bailing, after taking on water going through rapids

Back on the now calm river we relaxed as we went by a few huts. Not many settlers here. At the settlement of Santa Rosa a man came out to meet us and check our military papers. He signed our passports with a flourish and insisted we have a drink of national whiskey. National whiskey seems to be pure grain alcohol. It ripped its way down our empty stomachs and tried to come back up again. But, it is the custom. We smiled and drank.

Once back in the canoe, Al and Lenny tried to get Jose to camp on the right bank that night. Jay and I argued with them. "It's too dangerous. This is Auca territory."

"We have guns," Al said, brandishing the 22 caliber pistol."

"That's a pea shooter that won't do a lot of damage and you can't aim. The Aucas would have several spears through you before you even hit one," Jay and I said.

"I can aim," Al said. "I've been practicing all day." "I understand the thought processes of the natives," said Lenny. "I've talked to a few in the past few days and know I can make peace, even with wild ones, just through body language. If that fails, my 30-30 Winchester will settle the matter. The villagers will thank us for getting rid of a few Aucas, if it comes to that. Besides, you and Jay both have rifles."

"Just like the Canadian," we said.

Jay and I said no more. This is madness. It's the Auca's home. They know the jungle. We know nothing. I thought of Al trying to hold and aim that little pistol, let alone shoot it. He might panic and call for his mammy. An immature 18-year-old kid and a third year psychology student with delusions of grandeur were putting our lives on the line.

Lenny said to Jose, in poor Spanish, putting his hands together on the side of his head, "We sleep on the right bank (*al la derecha*) tonight," motioning with his right hand. Jose agreed most heartily. Then Lenny crawled up to the paddlers in front and again made motions to do the same. They, too, agreed. And smiled.

"It wouldn't bother me to drop off the two of them and we camp on the left side," I said to Jay. "We have too many psychiatrists now. Two less won't matter."

"We can drop them off tonight and pick them up in the morning," Jay offered.

"But not before a leisurely breakfast, let them settle in properly."

I was apprehensive about getting speared while letting them off. I uncased our rifles. Jose, at the tiller, looked puzzled. "*Por el Aucas*," I said.

"*Aucas al la derecha*," Jay said.

"*No vamous a la derecha*," Jose said, a little puzzled.

It was time to land. Lenny and Al had guns in hand and were standing up looking into the jungle when the paddlers spotted a good place to camp. Up went the paddles pointing left. Jose brought the helm around toward the left shore. Lenny was incensed. "*A la derecha*," he yelled, "*A la derecha!*"

Jose answered, "*Si, señor, si, señor,*" and landed our dugout on the left shore. These amiable Quechuas will agree to anything but do what is expedient. We were a few miles down river past Santa Rosa, ensconced on a large playa (beach) left when the winding, twisting Napo reversed its course. They put our duffles on the beach and we set up camp. Al started complaining, first about no trees to hang our hammocks from and then everything in general. He must be thinking of Ayn Rand's Atlas Shrugged, where we, the superior beings should be dominating the Aucas. Lenny didn't say much, just scowled, perturbed at not having power over the paddlers.

We cut bamboo sticks to hold up the hammock's mosquito netting and laboriously built a fire to heat water for coffee. All this took an hour, as none of us were experienced campers. The paddlers watched quietly, while eating *chicha*, (masticated yucca root chewed by women, spit into a bowl and left to ferment). In time the juice is poured off and the solids packed in leaves for travel. At mealtime they mix the substance with water and pack the solids back in the leaves. The white, milky juice is slightly alcoholic and not very tasty, but nourishing. It is the staple of their diet. Missionaries are distressed at the alcoholic content of the *chicha*. This boggled my mind. Wine is biblical, *chicha* is their life sustaining nourishment. Should they go hungry just to avoid alcohol? It all depends on how you parse a bible verse.

We finally boiled coffee and heated our last two cans of beef stew. We had planned to take shifts watching for Aucas all night, but didn't. Somehow the danger on our side of the river wasn't threatening, especially at night. We crawled into our sleeping bags and slept peacefully.

Monday, August 3, 1959 - Rio Napo, Ecuador
Next morning our pot was hanging on a tripod of bamboo sticks over a fire, thanks to the paddlers. The first demonstration of our inferiority. While the last of our oatmeal was cooking, (not nearly enough, but all we had left) Al was gone. "Where is

he?" I asked. Lenny and Jay shook their heads. I searched. He was some distance away, walking up and down the beach with a leather pouch and ribbon wound up his arm and another leather pouch tied to his forehead. I went back to the cooking oatmeal.

Later, when asked, he said, "It's a phylactery. I'm a conservative Jew. It contains the law of Moses we repeat while saying our morning prayers."

Our bags were in the dugout, the sky was clear and we set off on a much wider river free of eddies. No snakes, no charging beasts, no savages. Peaceful and quiet. We shed our shoes and much of our clothing.

Jungle village grass thatched chantey

Our passenger got off at a tiny village where a man was hacking away at a dugout canoe with an adz. We didn't get out, fearing he might offer us whiskey national.

As the day went on we tried fishing with tinfoil for bait. No luck. At noon, when the sun was directly overhead, amid much shouting and waving of paddles we pulled in near a pool. Jose lit three sticks of dynamite with a piece of punk, tossed it into the pool, then shoved off. It was a long fuse, more than two minutes.

"Kaboom." Water shot up in a fountain. Dead fish covered the surface of the pool.

"Not a bad way to fish," we said, "but illegal in Minnesota." They gathered the fish, but offered us none. We decided to delve into our large tin of peanuts, each man taking a handful. Our hands were not the same size. After this, we decided, one man would grab a handful for each one. Food became our prime topic of conversation. To "eat what the natives eat," wasn't working. We had not enough contact with the natives to trade for food.

Jack and the backdrop of an immense jungle

"*Lluvia*," Jose said. We looked at the clear sky, but put on our ponchos as he pulled into the left shore and made us a bamboo and leaf shelter. The rains came quickly and lasted two hours. As it cleared, each one of us hacked our way into the thick vines for several feet and yelled to find our way out again. The paddlers laughed. We thought, "How could the Aucas live in this dense forest? Who were they? Where did they come from? Why settle here?"

Al, my pistol in hand, walked along the bank looking for game, but fortunately found none. A 22 caliber bullet would irritate any animal enough to charge.

Down river another hour and it was time to camp. The paddlers built a fire and set up a tripod for us, knowing the stupid gringos needed all the help they could get. We made coffee and ate our last can of beans. Cane-like plants laid over the rocks made sleeping bearable but not comfortable. Al was bitching, unhappy in the real jungle. Up at dawn, camp at dusk, was to be our routine. The paddlers camped some distance from us.

Jack, Al and Jay making camp

A beautiful evening looking out over the serene Rio Napo

Tuesday, August 4, 1959 - Coca — Rio Napo, Ecuador

Coca, a small village of a few huts and one priest, is at the confluence of the Napo and Coca Rivers where Francisco de Orellana started his trip to the Amazon. Here, a kind priest lived in isolation. He sold us cigarettes, Ecuadorian and rice and gave us candy and dried milk, from U.S. government surplus. Neither the candy nor milk agreed with the native's digestive tract and had to be thrown away or used by Europeans. The good news was that the manufacturers got tax credits for these items shipped 2,000 miles at government expense to be discarded. The U.S. government works in mysterious ways. The priest asked a native woman to boil us a dozen eggs, "*durro*" (hard), rapping his knuckles on the desk to make the point, obviously sensing we were hungry. These were rationed out, one per man per day.

We watched native women sitting in a line, picking hair lice from the woman ahead of them. The first one in line had no hair to search and the last had no one to pick hers. I thought it would be better for them to sit in a circle, but what did I know? Jungle rats the size of dogs scavenged from the huts to the river.

Back on the river we had our handful of peanuts for lunch and talked about food, each recalling his favorite meal, who made it, who was there, what was served, what was discussed and what we did before and after the meal. No hurry, traveling through the jungle in a dugout canoe is not demanding. Each day is the same, ensconced by an 80-foot wall of green on either side.

My favorite meal was cooked by my mother with the help of Aunt Annie: Roast beef, mashed potatoes smothered in a delicious dark gravy, green beans, homemade bread sliced thick with butter churned by my father, cole slaw and cottage cheese on the side. One sister-in-law brought salad for the first course and the other brought homemade apple pie for dessert, served with a slice of ice cream made at Halgrens creamery where my father and one brother worked. Ah, there was good. Somehow just remembering food helped quench the hunger. Before the meal we talked to and about the children, now three in each family. After dessert we drank coffee and played the card game, 500, watching uncle Ray closely who tried to cheat, but always got caught.

Jay's meal was southern fried chicken, which he loved, prepared by his grandmother. She was from Texas. He didn't have to eat the okra. His father was raised in an orphanage and whatever wasn't eaten at one meal turned up on your plate on the next until you ate it. He didn't want to force this on his sons. Our descriptions of meals were more elaborate than I am recounting, but hunger makes food an obsession.

Years later, as a Swaggy, I often went hungry and kept a dollar bill folded in my billfold if I ran out of money. I learned to spend it all at once on a good meal with dessert and coffee for 55 cents and save enough for toast and coffee in the morning. To parcel it out one candy bar or dough-nut at a time just keeps you hungry. Once I went three days without anything to eat and found that after the second day I was no longer hungry. My body seemed to say, "I've been telling you I need food and you do nothing about it. Now I give up. You're on your own."

I can't remember Lenny's meal or who cooked it. Those attending were from his father's country club and the conversation evolved around money and the airplane his father had just purchased. Lenny had never worked up an appetite at hard labor so food had never been important. Their meal was finished off with a fine brandy.

Al outdid us all. His bar mitzvah had how many guests? 50? 100? More? And how many thousands of dollars did he receive? 100? 200? I was too overwhelmed to handle that many zeroes. The tables packed with food. The entertainer was cantor, a former opera singer. My roast beef, Jay's southern fried chicken and even Lenny's father's airplane was zeroed out. Al lived in a different world.

We continued to talk about food for the rest of the trip down river but in smaller items, maybe a White Castle hamburger, with a pot of beans, a Guess What candy surprise, jawbreakers, Eskimo pies, the abundant breakfast my mother fixed for us the day we left, Mrs. Conns' meatballs. To make matters worse we were running low on coffee.

The Napo River got wider and displayed a spacious grass covered beach on the left bank. This caught our attention – imagine, sleeping on soft grass instead of rocks and sticks. Then a garden, filled with pineapples and vegetables caught our eye. "*Primavera,*" (Spring) Jose said as he guided the canoe ashore. It looked like paradise. A beautiful *señorita*, smiling pleasantly came to greet us. "*Buenos dias, Señores,*" she said. I was hers, she could draw up the contract, include any conditions, demand anything. I was hers – but I had nothing to offer, not even cigarettes.

"*Buenos dias,*" We replied, and she took us to meet her husband, Otto Rodriquez.

Otto was a fine man, about 30, who hunted jaguars and knew some English. Their large jungle house with solid rough board sides and a grass roof was elevated on poles five feet above the ground to keep out snakes. Waist high bamboo slats enclosed the open-air front porch, which overlooked the river. Potted herbs surrounded the enclosure. A ladder ramp went up to an attic eight feet above the floor. Otto was building a guest house where the paddlers placed our belongings. No walls but a real treat to have a roof overhead. A large animal with a long snout was disturbed under the house and came out. Our first tapir sighting. Their pet. We gave him room.

It was late afternoon and, as was the custom, they would accommodate us for the night. Otto and his wife dressed neatly, he in a patterned shirt and trousers, she in dress and blouse, a lovely couple. They were independent, free from the restraints of civilized strife. With garden vegetables, chickens and game for food, what more could one want? My companions went down to the garden by the river. I looked out at the solid wall of jungle and the river and felt at ease. I wanted to stay. This jungle is beautiful. Let Jay, Al and Lenny go on without me. I'll stay. Maybe find a *señorita* and hunt jaguars for a living. Or maybe just a Quechua girl to help with the work and comfort me at night. My mind was wandering. I realized I had been in the jungle too long. But maybe not. What civilized place could be this beautiful? This serene? Why would I go back? Jungle land is free, what you clear is yours.

I asked Otto if I could stay for two weeks until the next mail-boat. "*Si, Señor.* You can stay for two weeks or two years. It will cost you nothing. I will teach you to hunt jaguars."

My mind filled with questions: Why did he choose this particular place? How many jaguars did he get and how much are the skins worth? How did he get them to market? Did he sell other animals? Monkeys? Snakes? Kinkajous? What about the Aucas? Jay, Al and Lenny returned. We washed in a basin and did what we could to fix up for dinner. *Hacienda Primavera* had also caught their fancy, they too wanted to stay.

The beautiful Mrs. Rodriquez served the four of us, but ate in the kitchen by herself. It is the custom. Had there been a woman with us we would all have eaten together. It reminded me of what a man in Quito told us. "You gringos don't know how to treat your women. That's why you have so many broken marriages. You don't let them serve."

She was a good cook. Fruit juices, chicken, rice, fried plantain, a delicious vegetable new to me, all topped off with fresh pineapple. Our paddlers slept and ate separately. We were Blanco, they Negro.

Otto's wife (I never knew her name) joined us for coffee. We asked Otto if we could stay another day or two. "*Si, Señores.* I will take you on a hunt." That was it. Otto brought out his guitar and sang beautifully, then handed it to me. I played and sang, but I was outclassed and gave it back. We listened to he and his wife fill the air with gentle music. Once away from cities, radio, television and noise, music becomes personal. You are next to the singers pouring out their hearts in song, supplemented by the jungle night cacophony. Ah, there is good! You know them. You trust them. You love them.

We slept in our hammocks slung from the guest house uprights. What comfort! This is living.

Wednesday, Aug. 5, 1959 - Primavera

After *café con leche* and fried dough we found the paddlers and bribed them ten *sucres* each to stay. They were in no hurry to go and happy to do so. Time for them was not measured by clocks, but by sunrise and sunset. A glance at the 12-hour sun in the sky told them everything.

We walked around *Hacienda Primavera* and the Quechua huts with fruit stacked on porches and skins hung to stretch and dry. Most *haciendas* on the Napo are poorly kept, fruit plants neglected and inhabitants existing day to day. Everything here was well cared for. They lived in abundance. Why couldn't everyone live like this, work hard and prosper on free land? *Quien sabe?*

We followed Otto through difficult trails, hoping he wouldn't get ahead and lose us. He cut the vines and growth with his machete. We got tangled and hacked violently. He ambled over fallen logs and mud-holes. We fell in. The baited jaguar cages were empty. Several snakes passed but weren't interested in us. One small snake, with his head four inches above the ground, crawled over my boot. Some were seven feet long but thin and small by jungle standards. We saw none hanging out of trees

Ubiquitous ants crawled up inside our trousers when we stopped. They didn't seem to bother Otto, maybe he knew something we didn't. Al took some pistol shots at monkeys in the tree-tops and got a disgusted look from Otto for alerting the whole jungle we were there. Otto cut big leafs, 7 feet high, 2 1/2 feet wide at the base, to tuck into our belts and let fall over our heads. Ten minutes later it rained. We pressed on.

An hour later Otto raised his arms for us to be quiet. He heard something and motioned for us to crouch down, pointing behind us to the right and indicating he would go around and chase whatever it was toward us from the rear. We hunkered down with our rifles at the ready and waited. I took my pistol back from Al, much to his disgust, and stuck it in my belt, afraid that a noise would incite him to pump off a few shots or hit Otto. He protested. I motioned for him to shut up and stay down.

Now we all heard the noise. Not loud, just branches and twigs being disturbed by something. I resolved not to fire until the last minute, worried about Otto. We could only see eight feet ahead on the trail, it would have to be one quick shot. But the jaguar never came. The noise went off to the side and Otto made sounds to let us know he was near. The beast had passed. I think if Otto had been alone he would have had it.

By a pool Otto made a strange sound by tapping his throat, calling otters. After a half hour we left, disappointed. We did, however, try to imitate the throat tapping sound. No luck.

Otto, Al and I were in the lead. Jay and Lenny dropped back to check their rifles. The trail wound through dense growth and soon we heard shouting and a gunshot. They were lost, 50 feet back.

Señor Rodriquez knew the jungle well. He could imitate the sound of any animal. Toucans lit on the trees near us and stared curiously. One toucan flew out of the dense growth, hovered in midair looking puzzled, and darted back in like open air was unfamiliar territory. Monkeys scrambled ahead, chattering in the treetops. Otto walked quietly, hacking his way through. We gringos stumbled along behind, noisily alerting the world of our presence. By the end of the day we were mud up to the waist, wet from the vegetation and covered with scratches. Otto was dry and unmussed. Back at the *Hacienda*, Otto apologized for finding no game and said it was a bad day for hunting. A real gentleman. We had experienced a day in the jungle.

"It's not at all what we expected," I ventured. "What are we going to tell the people back home?"

"Tell them what they want to hear," Lenny answered. He was already contriving hair-raising adventures.

Senor Otto Rodriquez and wife on their porch

Back at the *hacienda* Otto laid aside his rifle and showed us his blowgun, which he used for small game. He demonstrated. The hollow tube was 12-feet long. He cut a sliver of wood, 10 inches long from the slice of wood on his belt, wadded kapok around the dart to make it fit tightly, dipped it into the black, tar-like curare poison. With an antidote the animal can be kept alive. He indicated a knob 50 feet up on a tree and blew a dart into it.

Jaime Hedalgo, a river trader with an outboard motorboat arrived. Jay offered to sell him his rifle, he didn't like it and needed the money.

"I only have a few shells," Jay said. "They may be hard to find here."

"*Mio problema*," Jaime said, and they came to a quick agreement.

Jaime stayed for dinner and the night. Once again Otto's wife ate alone but joined us later for coffee and pineapple. Lenny made arrangements to buy more skins from him in Nuevo Roca*fuerte*, three days down river.

Guest chalet for river travelers

Jaime sang, Otto and his wife sang. What a pleasant way to spend the evening. Then Lenny had to take over. "Now a song from North America," he announced. "Everybody stand and link arms." Jay and I were embarrassed, knowing what was coming. Our polite hosts did as they were told.

"You put you left foot in, you put your left foot out, you put you left foot in and you shake it all about," he sang, kicking his foot in the air. Then the right foot, left arm, left hip and right hip followed. This stupid song, the "Hokey Pokey," went on and on. He had them doing his bidding, which he enjoyed. Jay and I quietly backed off. Finally it was over. Lenny was beaming.

Jaime turned his attention to Jay and me. Al had been quiet while at *Hacienda Primavera*, not really his world.

"Do you know about the Aucas?" he asked.

"We've heard a lot of stories about how savage they are," Jay answered. "But they live on the other side of the river and we are past their territory now, aren't we?"

"They live on the other side of the river, but move around. They are a constant threat. One waits outside a village for days until he sees a girl he wants, throws her over his shoulder and disappears into the jungle, or he throws babies up in the air and catches them on a spear." Jaime let this sink in, but we had heard it all before.

"A group of men along the river are going to wipe out one of the three tribes. They are looking for others to join them. If you are interested I can help you contact them."

"How about Rachael Saint?" we asked?

"Her group seems less violent now. The other two tribes are still savages. They plan to wipe out the worst one first then deal with the others later."

Jay said, "We will be back in North America. When is this set to happen?"

"December. Forty one men so far. Fathers who have lost daughters to rape and death, wives and families speared and mutilated and other men who want to get rid of the Aucas. They want to kill them all."

"Are you and Otto going?" I asked.

"Oh, no. We are settled with families."

Neither of us believed this but understood their risk of being found out. "We'll think about it," Jay said, wisely. Al and Lenny said nothing. We, of course, could not and would not come back for the slaughter. Jay had met Rachel Saint and she had helped us. What was our obligation to her? Should we tell her so she had time to save their souls before they died? We decided to stay out of it, watch the newspapers and listen to the missionary station on short wave for news of Ecuador.

Thursday, August 6, 1959 - Primavera, Rio Napo, Ecuador

After breakfast of fried dough and *café con leche*, Mrs. Otto offered us a local delicacy, several squirming fat worms, similar to Minnesota grub worms we used for fishing. We politely declined.

Jaime left. The Ottos gave us several souvenirs, panpipes, jaguar skulls, small things. While we were packing up, two men walked by carrying a long pole between them with a dozen chickens with tied legs, hanging upside down. We would scarcely have noticed except the pole broke and left them chasing chickens, our amusement for the day. Al tossed his rotting, stinking, salt-packed vampire bat into the river. Our paddlers had built a covered wagon type roof over our place in the canoe to replace the crude cover we had put up. It was beautifully made. Once again we realized we were ill suited for their environment and thanked them.

Senor Rodriquez with Lenny, Jay and Al holding his tigre (jaguar) skins

After many thanks and a sad farewell we shoved off. I, for one, was reluctant to leaver this paradise, but I am not a jungle man. Al was again up front with my pistol, taking pot shots at birds in the treetops and complaining about the lack of adventure. For lunch we had a handful of peanuts and fruits the Rodriquezs' had given us, saving the eggs and rice for the evening meal. I was the designated cook. While I was boiling rice and frying eggs someone complained and I, in a huff, resigned. I was generally irritated in and jumped at the chance to throw a fit. Lenny took over and did a good job considering what he had to work with. We washed the dishes with sand from the river.

Friday, August 7, 1959 - Rio Napo, Ecuador

After another night sleeping on bamboo poles laid over rocks, we just had coffee for breakfast. Al paraded up and down the beach with his phylactery on his wrist and forehead. We pressed on, the river was quiet and I felt nostalgic for *Primavera*. A man from a tiny settlement of a few huts waved us down and insisted he look at our papers. After an official examination, he signed each of them in an unreadable scrawl. Who was he? Who knows? I don't think he could read, but his neighbors were impressed. He offered us a shot of "whiskey national," which we could not refuse. God, how terrible it is! My throat burned all the way down to my stomach. We smiled graciously and wanted to trade for rice or eggs, but had nothing left to trade. Cigarettes, the best trading commodities, were all gone. I had purchased two cartons of Winstons in Quito, Jay only one. "If he runs out," I thought, "tough. He has to learn to plan ahead, especially in the jungle."

When that did happen, he didn't say a word about it or ask me for a smoke. After a day of this I knew what he was going through and shared mine. I didn't want to be in the same canoe under these circumstances, it would be like one of us having food and the other not. Now we were both out of cigarettes. Jose saw our predicament and showed us how to shred a tobacco-like plant and roll it up in plantain leaves. Tasted terrible but it did give smoke. Tobacco is a difficult habit to break. We thought of smoking rope, but weren't quite ready for that.

That night we camped on a wet sand bank. Jose said we would leave early in the morning, *"El grippe esta aqui"* (This is a place of sickness). Our clothes were rotting, my shirt-sleeves fell away, one leg dropped off Jay's pants and the seat of Lenny's pants was in tatters. Al's Brooks Brothers suit, which he was again wearing, was holding up well. I vowed to write to them and suggest they come out with a jungle line, which could open up a new market for them.

After a light meal of egg and a bit of stale bread, a man arrived with a stock of green bananas. We thanked him but had nothing to give in return. Lenny had picked this time to boil a jaguar skull from Otto for the teeth. The banana man inquired about it. Lenny, taking advantage of the situation, fabricated an elaborate story and told him, with much arm waving and stomping around, about the hunt for this huge jaguar and how he had constantly eluded us. Our visitor seemed to understand and listened intently. Lenny went on, saying the jaguar had circled around and was creeping up behind us. And then, while our backs were turned, he charged! By now all of us were listening, wondering how this wild tale would end. The banana man's eyes grew wider and he asked excitedly, *"Entonces, que passé?"* (Then, what happened?) Lenny calmly turned around and showed him the seat of his tattered pants. Our visitor laughed so hard he nearly fell into the fire.

We ate several bananas but we craved meat and potatoes.

Our sleeping bags and hammocks were so wet Lenny and I slept uncovered, vampire bats or no vampire bats. We again laid bamboo sticks to keep us off the wet sand, which was alive with small beetle–like creatures with claws like crabs. Several times we woke up thinking snakes or rodents only to find these little non-biting bugs. The jungle cacophony was boisterous, seeming to rejoice in our misery. This was my worst night on the Napo River. Still it was better than the mule trip.

Saturday, August 8, 1959 - Rio Napo, Ecuador

We each grabbed a couple bananas and left camp without building a fire. Jay complained of a pain in his liver. *El Grippe*? Or something more serious? He had a fever, a pain in his side and a feeling of weakness. We had no medicine. Jay lies in the bottom of the canoe and as the day went on the pain grew steadily worse.

"If I kack off just kick a hole in the sand and bury me, don't carry a dead, rotting body down river."

"Jose," we asked in our best Spanish, "Can we go faster, Jay is ill."

"The snail cannot go like the fish," he said, as near as we could make out, but he would try.

The only place that might have a doctor or medicine was *Nuevo Rocafuerte*. We might get there tomorrow night. We spread his sleeping bag and hammock to dry in the canoe so at least he could sleep dry tonight. For lunch Jay declined his handful of peanuts.

Drums sounded in the distance. I had heard drum beats in African movies but was surprised to hear them here. Do these natives also dance around a fire to a beating drum? Were we about to be attacked? Are we in danger? Do the Aucas have drums?

"*Que es el boom-boom*?" I asked Jose.

He listened carefully and said, in Spanish, "Four gringos come in canoe." We didn't know who or where they were, but we had been announced.

The paddlers did not stop all day, even for the rain, continuing on until the abrupt sunset made it too dark to see. Most of our stuff was damp. With no place to hang hammocks – the jungle formed a solid wall – we made Jay as comfortable as possible. Once again we had a couple bananas and slept, not bothering to boil coffee and not willing to ask the paddlers to sell us some of their *chicha*. We were not yet hungry enough to eat chewed up yucca spit into a bowl to ferment nor negligent enough to piss in the river, not wanting to cut off our *pirocas*. Outside of that we were dirty and disheveled, abluting ourselves in river water, having run out of wiping paper weeks ago. Is this what it means to "Go native?"

I lay awake, damp, listening to the jungle pandemonium; worried about Jay's *grippe* and wondering what the hell I was doing here while a nice warm bed in Minnesota lie empty. And Al? Al never helped out with camp work, that was for servants. We gave up trying to convince him, it was easier just to do it ourselves. At least he had stopped complaining. Lenny seemed to have become a part of the crew and, for the nonce, at least, was pleasant enough. Jay, of course, would die without complaint, not wanting to trouble the rest of us.

Monday, August 9, 1959 - Rio Napo, Ecuador

We awoke to the sound of a cyclone. It was some distance away but coming towards us at a tremendous clip. Everyone was up, even Jay, though he could hardly walk. Quickly rolling up our camp gear, we looked around for Jose. He was not to be found. Spreading out, we found them all downstream eating *chicha*.

"Hurry," we said in English. "Big wind coming. We have to get our stuff together and get out of here, quickly." We pointed at the sky, jumping around frantically. The paddlers were all laughing and kept dipping their fingers into the *chicha*. Jose smiled. "*Monos*," he said, pointing at the treetops.

"*Monos*? Monkeys? No, this is a tornado. Not monkeys."

He kept smiling. This bilingual conversation was not working. He had heard the noise and seemed unconcerned. "*Monos*?" we thought. The big noise went on for 10 or 15 minutes, not shaking any trees or blowing anything down. Howlers, we later found out, are large red monkeys with unusual vocal chords that resonate howling noise for several kilometers. They had us fooled.

Once again the paddlers worked hard. Jay lay in the bottom of the canoe and complained of a pain in his liver. Dirt and damp clung to us. We arrived at Tiputini and had to stop for a military check. The drums had heralded our arrival. The commander couldn't understand why Al had different papers than the rest of us, but let us pass.

Nuevo Rocafuerte is the last Ecuadorian village on the frontier, 15 miles from Peru. We were met by Carlos Chang and the young doctor with a host of villagers eager to greet the *Norte Americanos*. After the necessary introductions and greetings, Jay was taken to the dispensary, which consisted of two cots in a grass roofed hovel. Between the cots was a small monkey tied to a line nailed to the floor. This poor little animal had my sympathy.

The young doctor, an intern from Quito sent here to complete his training, was casual, smiling and friendly. He didn't know what Jay had, maybe the *grippe*, which covered a host of jungle diseases, but at a glance, prescribed a shot of penicillin, which we had to buy from Chang, the supplier of medicines and everything else. The doctor didn't think it necessary to sterilize the needle before giving Jay the shot, so we did it with matches. Chang explained, out of earshot, that Ecuadorian doctors were not highly skilled and the jungle was a good place to intern. "Here, if you make a mistake, you bury it and move on to the next patient." Not a comforting thought. Lenny and Al were already off somewhere wheeling and dealing. I got to know and like Chang. He had learned English at a mission school before having to leave China because of the Communist takeover and ended up here selling supplies brought up river by his Chinese trader friend.

He took me on a tour of the village, which was getting ready for the August 10th "Festival of Independence," the most celebrated holiday in Ecuador. Once a year they show a movie the day of the festival on a big sheet set up in the open air. Last year it was a Western and they were still talking about how low the hero had worn his guns and how fast he was on the draw. The locals carry pistols but do not have holsters. Instead they stick the gun in their belt, which has caused some accidents involving the *piroca*. This year it is to be a Tarzan movie, which will show more wild animals in two hours than these jungle dwellers will see in their lifetime.

Chang's river friend will not be back for some weeks and he didn't know when another boat would arrive. No one can remember any other *Norte Americanos* crossing the border to Peru here, not in the last 20 years at least. A constant state of hostilities has existed between the two countries for over a hundred years. An invasion by Peru in the 1940s was temporarily successful but ended with a treaty.

As we walked and talked, a young man with a snake around his arm attracted a crowd by showing his reptile smoke a cigarette. Then he got bit. The doctor, who was nearby, waved his hand, and told him to wash in the river.

Al and Lenny found me and announced they were leaving on the first boat out.

"What about Jay?" I asked.

"What can we do?" Lenny answered. "If he dies, they will bury him here. If he lives, he can make his way back to Quito. We have no reason to stay. Are you coming with us?"

I could not believe what I was hearing. "We've been together for two months in some difficult situations. Now you just want to leave him alone in the middle of the jungle?"

"There is nothing we can do to help him," Lenny replied. "I want to get back in time for school and Al's cousin is getting married in three weeks. He doesn't want to miss the wedding."

Al just shrugged his shoulders. Lenny, whom I now realized was a sociopath and cared for no one but himself, had complete control of him. "Are you coming with us or not?" he asked.

"No, I'm staying with Jay. You two go on ahead."

They left. I was relieved to be rid of them. Back at the dispensary Jay was sleeping and seemed to be breathing all right. I sat on the other cot for a while and tried to pet the monkey who would have none of it.

I found Chang and asked him about a knit shirt that could stretch to fit me and food and cigarettes. The shirt was okay, the Ecuadorian National cigarette tasted awful. "You can eat with me," he said and took me to his neighbor's place. "She makes chicken, I love chicken."

It was good. I took a plate to Jay. He could sit up enough to eat a little, but was still very ill and lay back down. Room and board at the visitor's hovel cost 25 *sucres* per day but Chang said I could stay with him and eat at his neighbors for 10 *sucres* per day. "Lenny and Al are leaving," I said, "so it will just be Jay and me until he gets well enough to travel."

"They will not leave," Chang said. "There is no boat available and the border is closed for the festival. My river man will be back from Iquitos in three or four weeks. He will take you into Peru in his small boat. After that you can book passage on a launch to Iquitos."

"Is that the only way?"

"Yes, unless *Señor* Pando lets you take his launch to Pantoja."

Señor Pando was mayor, or something, of Nuevo Rocafuerte. He seemed our best chance of getting across the border. I resolved to ask him in the morning.

"But don't leave," Chang continued. "I will take you hunting and fishing. We will catch *pañas* (piranhas) and shoot cayman (relative of the crocodile), we'll have a good time. Stay," he said, almost imploringly. He liked me, was probably bored being isolated here and needed some new company. Staying with Chang was tempting but three or four weeks were too long.

I took some cigarettes to Jay, probably not a good idea, but it might help him pass the time. I said nothing about Al and Lenny leaving, he had enough to worry about. The doctor came to check on his patient and said Jay had hepatitis or pneumonia and would be well enough to travel in three days. Things were looking up. I asked him about the monkey. "I bought him for my nephew in Quito."

"Are you interested in selling him?" I asked. I would like to buy him for my nephew in Minnesota. Maybe you could purchase another?"

"Oh, no. I could not sell him."

So the monkey would stay chained to the floor for how long? Three or four months? Eating the few scraps thrown to him and living in his own feces? But it was his decision. Chang was becoming a friend and he knew the doctor.

"Wait until tomorrow and offer him a price."

"I haven't seen our paddlers. Are they still here?" I asked. "I would like to say muchas gracias and bid *adios*."

"They will stay for the fiesta, spend all their money on *cerveza* (beer) and *putas* (loose women) then paddle back up river. You probably won't see them again," he said with a smile.

A crowd was gathering in the village and snare drums announced the army marching in from Tiputini, a few miles upstream. They were trying to keep in step, but a glance made me hope I never had to rely on them. Lenny showed up with Al and said they decided to stay together with us, for the sake of everyone. I nodded in agreement. Again I'm stuck with the two of them. Lenny had found a pair of pants, too small, and was carrying a guitar, which he did not know how to play.

The population of Nuevo Rocafuerte is about 200. During the festival it swelled to 250 with the soldiers, their wives and families. Rocafuerte is an important city, a soldier told us, because it has a telephone.

"Where does the telephone go, *señor*?" we asked, "to Quito?"

"It goes to Tiputini."

"Oh, and from there to Quito?"

"No. From there it goes back to Rocafuerte."

The music contest started. First the village singers and then the soldiers sang with much applauding and yelling after each song. *Señor* Pando would decide the winner. Then, in the middle of all this, Lenny walked up and said something to the announcer, who looked at me. This was not our festival, nor our holiday, but Lenny always had to be the center of attention. We had tried singing together a couple times. Lenny could carry a tune but had no idea how to blend. Then he handed me the guitar, which I quickly tuned while we were announced. "*Entonces, Norte Americanos cantan* 'Rrrrrock 'n Rrrroll.'" ("Now North Americans will sing 'Rock 'n Roll.'") We sang, "I've Never Felt More Like Singing the Blues," with me harmonizing as well as possible. When it was over, they applauded politely and Lenny beamed and bowed. Rock 'n Roll just didn't fit in with the beautiful songs they had sung for generations. I was glad our part was over and we could listen to their wonderful singing, but wondered if Lenny thought we might win the contest.

The contest got more and more heated after each song between the rival groups. It looked like trouble for *Señor* Pando. He had to pick a winner. I looked around for the fastest way out of the town square if pandemonium broke out. Tension filled the air. After this hour and a half contest, *Señor* Pando stood up, complimented the army singers to much applause, acknowledged the town singers and praised them to much applause and said he wanted to hear each group again before deciding. He went back and forth mentioning the strong points of each group, then stood up straight, looked at all of us carefully and announced, with the wisdom of Solomon, "These two groups are the best singers in all of Ecuador. It would be impossible to select a winner. Both will receive first prize."

Ecuadorian Army, at ease

Señor Pando was a true politician. I was hoping he would still be in good spirits when we visited him in the morning. The crowd started jubilantly dancing in the street. Carlos Chang later told us the contest always ended in a tie. "I will jump in the river and swim upstream and die for Ecuador," one soldier said, waving his bottle of beer in the air, before falling down drunk. Several others were too far gone to walk. Then it was time for the movie.

Ecuadorian army, after watching Tarzan movie

The locals thoroughly enjoyed "Tarzan," dubbed in Spanish, swinging through the jungle from vine to vine and living in a tree house. There are no chimpanzees or elephants in South America, just monkeys and tapirs so Cheeta and Tantar were a big hit. I had a beer and left to avoid the revelry, which would go on all night and into the next day, and stopped at the dispensary to see how Jay was doing. He was awake after getting up to ask a drunken soldier, who had sacked out in the next cot, to leave. It was not enough to ask, he had to push him through the door, which led into the doctor's office where he stumbled over the doctor who was on the floor, having a dalliance with one of the local women. Jay had just returned to his cot as I arrived. Seems snakes in the trees weren't the only things you had to avoid in the jungle.

Monday, August 10, 1959 - Nuevo Rocafuerte

Al and Lenny slept in the school house for 25 *sucres* a day. I stayed with Chang for ten. He wanted nothing to do with *Señor* Pando so the three of us went to see *Señor* Pando about his launch. He spoke too loud and fast to understand. "*Por favor,*" I said, "*Hable más despacio.*" (Please speak more slowly). But he was a politician and spoke louder and faster. The border was closed today because of the festival, but we got the idea that he, Pando and the governor of the state, who was here to attend the fiesta, were leaving *mañana* in his launch and would be gone for several days. He dismissed us abruptly and left.

Much of the festival got rained out, but basketball, volleyball and races were held between storms. Jay had pneumonia, according to the doctor but thought he would feel well enough to travel in a day or two.

The day was quiet after last night's jubilation. The hungover army trudged back to Tiputini in disorder, leaving some inanimate colleagues on the roadside. The festival was over. Nuevo Rocafuerte would not see such an event for another year. Tarzan and Jane are now a part of their fiesta memories along with last year's gunslinger that carried his pistols low for a fast draw.

Tuesday, August 11, 1959 - Nuevo Rocafuerte, Ecuador
    I spent the night in Chang's residence and ate at his neighbor's house, the local restaurant. He was not surprised that *Señor* Pando, with the only launch in the village, made no effort to help us. This morning Jay was well enough to be up and about so Chang took us all to the Peruvian border in his canoe. The gracious Peruvians, reputedly the most cultivated and industrious in the Oriente, were often referred to as the Germans of South America. They cleared us to pass with a polite smile. Back at the village, Carlos Chang said his father-in-law had a motor canoe and could take us to Pantoja for 150 *sucres* ($11.25). Ah, what would we have done without him? Chang and I had become friends. I would have liked to know why he selected this village and this life, but I didn't want to pry. He was a good man.
    At Chang's suggestion I offered the doctor 80 *sucres* ($6) for his little squirrel monkey and he was mine. His name was Wiki, "crying one." I was overjoyed to have this cute little companion. His collar went around his waist, just in front of his hind legs. Riding on my shoulder he caught flies deftly with his fast little hand and bit my ear lobe regularly if I moved too quickly or did something he didn't like. He defecated often, on me. My shoulder, my lap, and sometimes my head. Nine times in the first hour. This took some getting used to and necessitated repeated washings. I attributed this to his nervousness in new circumstances and hoped he would get better. He didn't for the first few days.
    Lenny, not to be outdone, bought a tiny monkey that looked like a rodent. This was too much for Jay, who seldom took issue with anything or complained. "What are you going to do with those stinking varmints? We came here to experience the jungle, not take it home with us. You'll be covered with excrement (my word, not

his) the rest of the trip. Just keep those damn critters away from me." I knew now he was feeling better and would be back to normal in a few days, if we kept the monkeys away from him.

The friendly townspeople heard we were leaving on the morrow and bid us farewell with several offers of "whiskey national." To refuse the best they had to offer would be an insult, so we did our duty. The choice between "whiskey national" and kerosene would be a toss up. We flopped into our sleeping bags on Chang's floor, inebriated.

Wednesday, August 12, 1959 - Nuevo Rocafuerte, Ecuador

After *café con leche* and fried dough we tossed our baggage into Chang's father-in-law's motor canoe. Our possessions were growing – skins, native made hammocks, native panpipes, carvings, and pieces of junk. Al had tossed his vampire bat but now had large shoots of bamboo, carved wood, jaguar skulls and God only knows what else to show his family back in Birmingham. The large canoe was packed to the gunwales, with no room for Chang. It could easily sink, I thought, but if it did, we would be free of a lot of rubbish we no longer needed. I thanked Chang and wished him well, knowing I would never see him again and we pushed off. The villagers waved us *adios* from the shore. Meeting *Norte Americanos*, aka *Gringos*, was a big event for them. Fortunately, the river was calm. Carlos Chang's father-in-law delivered us safely to the Ecuadorian army camp across the river from Pantoja, the Peruvian army's camp. We planned to hire another dugout canoe to take us down river to Iquitos and expected it to cost $60 to $80.

Wiki was nervous and I was covered with feces when we landed. I just dived in the river and scrubbed, being careful not to piss, for fear of losing my *piroca*. We could see the Peruvian's with tommy guns having target practice. Our soldiers looked apprehensive knowing it would be a short battle if the Peruvians attacked, as they only had old rifles. This armed border conflict had been going on for more than a hundred years, the latest battle had been resolved in 1942, but the war was on the edge of flaring up again.

Jay and I looked at our maps, but found no place names. We had no idea where we were. The Peruvian army launch had just left. We were told another was due in a few days on which we could book passage to Iquitos. Good news, we wouldn't have to travel by canoe anymore.

This camp of about 50 soldiers and wives was set a small clearing. Walk 30 feet in any direction and you are in the jungle. We were given a grass-roofed hut on stilts. Every settlement has at least one for visitors, with table, chairs and room to hang our hammocks. What luxury. Jay and I relaxed and smoked available Ecuadorian cigarettes, which tasted awful. I peeled one open out of curiosity to see the tobacco. It was moldy! Covered with fungus! We resolved to quit – someday – and resumed inhaling.

Presently our waiter, a soldier, arrived with four tin plates and four serving dishes filled with boiled yucca, baked yucca, rice and baked plantains. He set the food on the table, smiled and left. We were hungry but there is only so much starch you can pack in. Some yucca was left when he returned. He looked at it and shook his head in disappointment. "*No le gusta la comeda,*" (you don't like the food) he said as he picked up the plates. Rather than insult our host we decided to eat everything next time.

We were free to wander around the camp and found a balance scale. Jay had lost 32 pounds, I lost 25. Neither of us had been overweight when we left home.

August 13, 14, 1959 - Ecuador Army Camp
*   across the Napo River from Pantoja, Peru.*
After fried dough and delicious coffee, the four of us went different directions, knowing lunch was at noon. The soldiers

and their wives or maybe girlfriends, (Latin American armies never deprive their soldiers of the opposite sex) were easy going and friendly. With little to do, except be prepared for an invasion from Peru, they offered to take me on a hunt. We communicated by sign language. No point in asking Jay, he had sold his rifle. We walked the well-trodden jungle trails for a couple hours. This area was nearly hunted out as the only meat they got came from hunting. I took aim at a big bird in the treetop, but my soldiers said *"No vale"* (no value, not good to eat). Later I hit a bird at a distance, which surprised me, as I'm not a good shot. My soldiers were impressed. Their rifles misfired half the time. One bird was all we got, just enough to toss into a soup to feed 50.

For lunch we got the same as the night before, but divided each serving plate into quarters. Each of us was required to eat his share. When our waiter/soldier returned he was pleased and smiled graciously as he left. We were proud of having done the courteous thing only to have him return with four more serving plates of the same.

The food for these three days was basically the same, sometimes accompanied by a potato soup. Once we had *chicha*. I tried not to imagine the soldier's wives chewing yucca and spitting into a wooden bowl to ferment. Perhaps the fermentation made it safe to eat, or maybe the natives had built up immunity. It was drinkable, somewhat alcoholic. Whatever the case, we survived. The cookbook for the army must be quite limited.

The soldiers managed to bag a small deer, so we got a few meaty neck bones one night. I'm sure the officers got the steaks. Why didn't they raise a few chickens? Only the army knows. The butcher intrigued Lenny. "He skinned the deer by making only one cut in the stomach, and kept the hide in one piece. "

Lenny bought another monkey. It looked like a small gorilla. Still young it might make a nice pet, good natured, didn't bite or jump around and liked to be stroked, which Wiki didn't. Lenny's monkey was too large to sit on his shoulder whereas Wiki sat on my hand.

Jay was becoming quite fluent in Spanish and this was a good time to practice with the officers and enlisted men. This also gave a couple of them the chance to speak English. One in particular, Emilo, hated it here and wanted to come to the U.S. desperately. Each conversation with him ended in "equality."

Al went piranha fishing with a soldier. "He took me to a quiet pond and stood in knee-deep water, baiting our hooks with raw meat from snakes or lizards or something, then got back in the canoe to fish. The water roiled as they bit." Al was ecstatic at having experienced this entirely on his own. The half dozen fish he showed us were the size of large sunfish and had razor sharp triangular teeth, capable of stripping the carcass off a large animal in a few minutes.

"Why didn't the piranhas eat the bare legged soldier in the water?"

"He said blood or fast movement incited them to attack. If you weren't bleeding and moved slowly you were safe." I had my doubts.

As I suspected, Al planned to pack them in salt and take them back to Birmingham to show these swimming man-eaters to his relatives.

After an afternoon of cayman hunting (seeing none) up the murky Yasuni River we settled in to await the launch to Iquitos. The jungle army camp was boring. I concurred with Emilo who wanted to leave and go to the United States.

Wiki had acclimated somewhat, leaving me almost presentable. His line, tied to my wrist, was long enough for him to jump off my shoulder to defecate. Lenny's was more considerate. I liked his monkey, not yet named.

Saturday, August 15, 1959 -
  Boat on the Napo River in Peru to Iquitos, Peru
Our launch arrived but would stay for only a couple hours. Al was off *piraña* fishing.

"It'll take a while to load," he said. "I'll be back in plenty of time."

We left Al's bags on shore, just in case. We no longer gave a damn, as he was getting too arrogant. We boarded the Ecuadorian boat to take us across to Pantoja. Emilo waved and cried "Equality" as we shoved off.

The launch was larger than I expected. Our rooms were on the upper deck, as we were Blancos. The lower deck was filled with chickens, dead and alive pigs, parrots, turtles, 5 monkeys and 70 soldiers. I didn't think the camp had that many. The departing soldiers were assigned to a raft fastened to the side of the launch, their wives and children stayed on the lower deck, sleeping in hammocks or on the deck. There weren't enough toilet facilities but the Napo flows fast and can handle effluence.

We were just casting off when Al arrived via canoe. The launch captain paused while Al, smiling arrogantly, and his baggage came aboard. "I had to leave the *pirañas* we caught this morning," he said. "They're edible."

"Too bad," I said, sarcastically. "I heard they go well with *chicha*. Now we're stuck with chicken and pork."

A nicely dressed young man informed us we would arrive in Iquitos in five or ten days, depending on circumstances, and would not be allowed off the boat until then.

"What if it sinks?" I wanted to ask as a joke, but kept my mouth shut. Our first class fare, including meals, was 150 Peruvian *soles* each ($5.25). The *camarote* (cabin) cost 50 *Soles* ($1.75) each. He showed us our room with innerspring mattresses. Ah, this is living. Two women were sitting on the floor just outside our door. Jay and I looked at each other.

"Do they have rooms?"

"No, they will be fine on deck."

"Let them have our room, we'll sleep on the deck, we're used to it." The young man said something to them, in Quechua, and they left. He smiled.

"*Esta bien*," he said and walked away.

We said no more, not wanting to mess with a system that worked for them. Lenny and Al were in similar quarters. We met two middle-aged officers with large bellies (a sign of success) who introduced themselves. The two beautiful young women at their sides (another sign of success) were gracious and well mannered, obviously their wives were home taking care of the children. It is an acceptable way of life to everybody, and it works, I thought, but not in the States. American wives would say, "Save it all up till you get home."

Our struggle was over; this was a life of ease. We were dry and warm. Jay felt better. We could see the jungle, but not feel it. Wiki settled in and I unsnapped the line from his waist collar and let him run loose. He couldn't get off the boat without swimming and his breed of monkeys do not swim. The overhead pipes had spiders and insects, he was back in the wild. I closed him in the room during meal time (his table manners were appalling), but outside of that he was free to roam, nobody minded. The crew cleaned up after all the animals on board. The launch was casual, to say the least.

Ah, the meals; soup, meat, potatoes, bread, plantains, yucca, pineapple and fruits, and butter. Canned butter. No refrigeration here. I had never seen nor heard of canned butter before. It was delicious. Our table seated the army officers, their mistresses and the launch captain. These beautiful young women smiled enticingly at us, scroungy, bearded, unbathed, clad in dirty, tattered clothes though we were. They were professionals.

I later asked one of the crew who spoke English "What happens when they age and are replaced by younger girls?"

"They marry and raise a family," he said.

I pressed the issue. "Would you marry a courtesan?"

"Of course, if she had saved her money and was ready to settle down. I am not climbing up in society so I do not have to have a woman, perhaps ugly, untouched by another man. If you move to another city no one will know. They might suspect, but will not know. Her former patrons will not reveal her identity. They are gentlemen and will behave as such."

He turned and looked at me directly.

"She knows how to please a man. She has only sold her body and in so doing has learned loyalty, manners and the rules of society. It's not like selling your whole being, body and soul, to a large corporation, which takes all and gives you a pittance in return. Here it is an acceptable profession. It is a way out for beautiful girls who otherwise are saddled with a drunken husband, poverty and half dozen children before the age of 30. Instead she has become a beautiful, mature woman with savings and knowledge of life a man will be happy to share. And she will understand if you visit *putas* (prostitutes) as a diversion."

He looked at the two courtesans. I did also, seeing them in a new light. I was beginning to understand a different culture, another way of life.

"The answer to your question is yes," he said as he walked toward the two ladies. Planning ahead, I thought. "Yes," I muttered to myself, "a different culture, not based on prosperity or power, that has some interesting benefits."

Sunday – Wednesday, August 16 –19, 1959
   Launch on the Rio Napo in Peru

The trip down the Napo River to the Amazon was calm and relaxing, more pleasant than if we had to hire another dugout canoe with paddlers or maybe paddle ourselves. How easily we are corrupted into indolence. Wiki adjusted quickly and liked to sit on my shoulder as long as he was free to choose. Jay was being barraged by the officer who was reading a volume on "*Norte Americanos*." He talked about it endlessly. Jay hardly got a chance to practice his Spanish.

But Lenny! Lenny came up to us with his little woolly Monkey on his arm, the best natured and best looking monkey we had seen.

"He's sick. He'll die tonight."

Al nodded his head in agreement.

"He looks okay to me, let me hold him a while," I said.

" No," Lenny said, pulling back. "He might have something serious that's contagious."

"At least let me pet him."

"No. He's dying. He will die tonight. I might have him stuffed."

"Wait and see how he does. He might get well."

My words fell on deaf ears. Lenny and Al walked away and I didn't think any more about it.

The next morning as Jay and I were coming to breakfast we met Lenny and Al. Lenny held a skin in his hand. "He died last night."

"Lenny skinned him by only making one cut in his belly," Al said proudly and spread the skin out.

This is madness, I thought to myself. He killed his monkey to have him stuffed, but I said nothing. Lenny showed us the skin, smiling, then casually tossed it overboard.

I tried to enjoy the trip and forget about Lenny but I kept a closer watch on Wiki, you never know.

One of the soldiers offered to buy my 22-caliber pistol and shells for 1,650 Peruvian *soles* (about $60). I knew he could sell it for more, but I needed the money. He pocketed the shells and stuck the pistol in his belt just above his *piroca*. I looked apprehensive. He said "*mio problema*" (my problem) and smiled. He, like many machismos in Peru, liked to live dangerously. I thought he might even piss in the river to show his courage.

Jay had done an admirable job of planning the trip and expenses. I had $290 left out of my original $620. The trip had not been over budget so far, but now being in Iquitos and flying home might leave us wanting for funds. Both Al and Lenny had family money behind them. Jay and I, from middle-class working families, had no one to bail us out. We could end up selling lottery tickets or stolen watches like street people here or maybe go into the jungle searching for cocaine. We'd make out, one way or another.

~~~
# ~ Part Three: Arrive ~
~~~

Wednesday – August 19 to 30, 1959 - Iquitos, Peru

We docked in Iquitos on the 19th, disembarked the next morning and checked into the Hotel Victoria for less than a dollar each per night. This luxury hotel had warm running water. You could stand under it in a stall and feel it pouring over your head. This water, with soap, washed nearly three months of packed grime off your skin and down the drain. Running water that you could piss in and not endanger your *piroca*, and a hotel laundry to wash your clothes. And beds with springs. Ah, what memories this brought back of "Minnesota clean." This is living! Would I trade this for *Primavera*? Would I ever again want adventure that involved the misery of crossing the Andes by mule? Or the discomfort of sleeping on rocks by a jungle river? No! Not ever again!

But how quickly we forget pain and misery. Once back in the comfort of Minnesota, Jay and I talked about crossing the Atlantic in a hot air balloon, surviving on a deserted island, prospecting for gold or uranium and other pursuits. Still, the thought of going back into the jungle was too fresh to reconsider and would have to wait; but perhaps, just perhaps.

A large white ship caught our attention. Jay and I sought out the ticket office and found two men dressed in white.

"Do you speak English?" Jay asked one of them. He looked at us curiously and offered, in the King's English, "If you speak slowly and enunciate clearly I will attempt to fathom your meaning."

"Does that mean 'yes'?" I asked, trying to lessen our show of ignorance with humor. He smiled.

Docked at the city of Iquitos, Peru, located in the middle of the Jungle

"The ship is of the White Star Line, a tourist ship and very expensive. Our office mainly books Cook's Travels, taking tourists, 8 to 10 at a time, on motorized trips to native jungle villages."

"That is not for us. We've been there. We are looking for a way back to the states. Any ships going that way?"

"Not from Iquitos. If you have time you may find river boats and get to Belem, then pick up a freighter. But it is a long, slow trip."

"Is there any other way out of here?"

"Iquitos was built for the rubber barons, but that's over. We are a big city in the middle of the jungle with no roads in or out except the concrete highway to the rosewood oil plant. The oil is shipped to perfumeries all over the world. Another boat won't be in for a month or so. But relax you will enjoy it here."

We stood wondering. He continued: "The big Iron house by the town square was built by Eiffel for the 1889 Paris fair. Bought by a rubber baron it was disassembled and shipped to Peru. However, the buyer lost it in a shipboard poker game. The winner had it carried through the jungle, piece by piece, by hundreds of men and now it stands on the town square."

"Many interesting things in Iquitos," the other said. "The two dozen Europeans living here do not like each other and are constantly bickering about something or other. We try to avoid them."

The other man joined in the conversation. "Herman Jesson has a thriving export business with native tribes making artificial orchids for him to sell in America."

"Yes," the first man said, "and each orchid stem is filled with cocaine; that's where the profit is. He was a judge in the Miss Universe contest. But you also must meet Charlie, he wrestles with snakes."

We chatted and left. Back at the hotel we met Al and Lenny for dinner. What luxury, a tablecloth and four waiters. After carefully looking at the Spanish menu we all ordered *bistec hidago*, rice and beans. *Bistec* must mean beefsteak. What cut we didn't care. A nice thick, juicy, steak was what we needed after two months on scant rations. They didn't ask how we wanted our steaks done, rare or medium, but that didn't matter. We'd eat them however they came.

The plates our waiters set before us were a surprise. *Bistec*, we learned the hard way, means fried. *Hidago* is liver. So we sunk our teeth into a thick slab of fried liver, resolving to learn more Spanish menu words.

We were stuck here. For the next few days we combed the docks for riverboats and I talked to Herman L. Jesson, the artificial orchid man, at Casilla 384. Herman flew in on a private plane and the owner of the plane lived in the same house. Jesson walked or canoed into the jungle searching for isolated, unknown Indians and showed me photos of tribes that pierced and tattooed their bodies and mutilated themselves in other ways, some men had bones stuck through their *pirocas*. He had walked through the jungles of Borneo as well as Brazil and Ecuador.

"Do you need any help on these trips? I would like go with you."

"Yes, you could come along. It would cost $1,000," he answered.

This, as he knew, was more than I could afford. I asked him

more questions but never found out why he did what he did or how he made money doing it. He was well established in Los Angeles and showed me his photo with Miss Universe. The only thing that fit was the cocaine in the stems of the artificial orchids. I became uncomfortable after chatting for a time. I thanked him and left, feeling there was something odious about him and his pilot, who hadn't said much.

How do we get out of here? *Quien sabe?* We spent days independently touring the city by foot, no cars here, and seeing what sights there were to see, meeting for dinner back at the hotel. Al was elated to tell us, on the second day, that he had been playing tennis.

"Where did you find a tennis court?"

"My friends, Josh and Saul, have a court. I can play anytime." Al had already found the Jewish community.

"Who are they? What do they do here?"

"They're businessmen and stay here part of the year, then go back to Europe," he answered.

"What kind of business?" I asked. "Traders? Import, export? What?"

Al just shrugged his shoulders. I knew we were not to meet these businessmen. Just as well, I don't know how to play tennis.

"Can they get us out of here?"

"No. They fly here in a private plane."

Lenny said little about his days. He left in the morning, came back for dinner and sometimes left again. One day he returned with a kinkajou, a ferret like nocturnal animal with a prehensile tail. The kinkajou, if held, had the habit of sticking its long tongue in your ear searching for insects.

The three of us visited Charles D. Hawkshead, a young herpetologist from Louisiana, here exporting animals and birds. He was happy to see us, as there were few people here to talk to. We had met several Europeans on the streets who tried to get us away from the other Europeans. We didn't want to get into this internecine affair. Charlie was interested mainly in snakes and alligators.

"I went to my senior high prom with an alligator as my date," he said. "The narrow minded bastards kicked us out. That's why I came down here, Peruvians are more open minded and accepting." He brought out a large gunnysack, saying, "This is a record size water boa," as he dumped it on the cement floor. Al almost knocked Jay and I over to get out the door, then drew himself up and said, "Give him room to work." We did, as Charlie pinned the snake's head to the floor and picked it up. The huge snake, a 17-foot boa constrictor, wrapped his body tightly around Charlie and squeezed. Charlie's assistant looked apprehensive but did nothing, awaiting Charlie's instructions. After coming close to us with the snake's head held in his hands, Charlie disentangled himself and put the snake back in the bag. We were impressed, but I'm sure he did this for every visitor.

There were animals of various kinds. Thirty or so marmosets, sitting in a cage, watched us together, turning heads in unison as we moved, unnerving. Caymans, ant eaters, monkeys and a host of others.

"It must be quite a job to feed them all."

"I have help. The night feedings are the most important for the nocturnal animals. Snakes are easy, they only eat every six months."

"Where do you find them all?"

"Through that door," he said pointing at the street. People bring them in daily, mostly boys who know their way through the jungle."

I started thinking. I'm not going to keep the monkey myself. I have two brothers with families and only one monkey.

"Do you sell any animals here, or do they all get shipped back to the states?"

"There is no market here, just go into the jungle and grab

what you want," he said.

"I'm not good at the jungle. Would you sell me a small mon-key?" I asked.

"Not another one," Jay said. "One is too many. Between you and Lenny we won't be able to get on a plane."

"They're for my nieces and nephews. I should bring them something."

"Why not something already dead, like a piranha or a vam-pire bat packed in salt? Do like Al," Jay continued.

"I had to throw mine," Al said. "They stunk"

I turned back to Charlie.

"They're prorated," Charlie said. "My partners back in the states don't want me to sell them for less. Which one do you want?"

I pointed at a squirrel monkey like Wiki, but white, almost albino.

"That one is $15. A good price, you'd pay $50 for him back home."

I looked at Charlie's assistant, Alberto. He showed five fingers surreptitiously.

"If you sell him here you'll save shipping costs. I'll give you $5."

"No, he goes for $15."

I'm not good at haggling and I wanted this cute little monkey. "Toss in a cage," I said. I'll be back tomorrow with travelers checks.

The next day Charlie was not there. Alberto said he was in bed with Miss Peru. We had heard she was in town on a promo-tion. I came back later with the checks.

"Miss Peru?" I asked. "She is available?"

"For a price," he said, with a smile.

"Quite a step up from an alligator," I thought.

Back at the Victoria Hotel the four little beasts adjusted to each other without squabble. Wiki, by now, had resigned himself to the inevitability of domestic life.

One day Lenny thought of something that led to competing. He liked to compete, even though he always lost, and challenged me to a race down to the next block. Three quarters of the way down I was a couple steps ahead and he fell on the concrete sidewalk. He would rather skin himself up than lose.

People gathered in the park at night. Young people walked around the square, *señoritas* one way, *señores* the other, assessing each other. Chaperones accompanied the girls. One night Lenny turned and joined a *señorita* going the other way. After a round or two he came back to us.

"Al is going to sleep in your room tonight. This young lady has agreed to spend the night with me," he said arrogantly.

"That's okay with us," we replied. He didn't know that while the *señorita* will agree to anything verbally, her two older aunts and younger brother, following some distance behind, would also come along. Jay told Al not to worry, he would have his own bed, and we went back to the hotel. It was not spoken of again.

One afternoon Jay, while taking a nap, was awaked by a thumping on the floor and yowling. Al was banging a lumpy gunnysack on the floor. Jay said, "What are you doing?"

"I can't do it," Al said.

"You can't do what?" Jay asked.

"I can't knock this cat out. Lenny is skinning cats."

"Lenny is skinning live cats?"

"Oh, no. We knock them out first."

"Get that out of here and stop this nonsense."

When Jay told me about this we looked around and found several cat skins drying on the tile roofs outside the hallway windows. He had broken some tiles placing them. One had been patched. We might get kicked out of here. Iquitos is full of stray cats, but where did he skin them? And what was he going to do with the skins once they were dried? I left it up to Jay to talk to Al and Lenny. If I confronted him it might get physical.

Walking down the street a boy approached us with a tiny two-toed sloth hanging from a stick by his prehensile tail. "Gracias, no quiero," I said. (Thank you, I'm not interested).

Lenny said, "*Cuantos cuesta*?" (How much). He bought the sloth for half that much.

"What are you going to do with that?" Jay asked, knowing the answer would be bizarre.

"A scientific experiment, which I will write up for a term paper. I'll fill a gallon tin with water, leave an inch of air at the top and seal the cover. Next day I'll do an autopsy to determine whether the sloth died of drowning or suffocation."

"No you won't," I said.

"It's my sloth," he said, "I'll do what I want with it."

I grabbed his arm and spun him around and was about to slug him when he threw the sloth back to the boy. Lenny was strange, sadist as well as a sociopath, and we were stuck with him till we got back to the states. I vowed next time I would just slug him, but for now would avoid him as much as possible.

I wanted to get out of here. Jay and I went to see Herman Jesson hoping to catch a ride somewhere with his pilot. Mr. Jesson was spurious, but his pilot struck us as a total fraud.

"Yes, I'm going to Barranquilla on the 30th and you can come along," he said.

"Great. How much do you charge?"

"$120."

"Good, we'll take it."

"Each." He was a man of few words.

"Each?" we thought. "For a short trip? He's gouging us mercilessly." We looked at each other. Herman said, "There's no other way. You might be stuck here for another month or two."

He was right. We reluctantly accepted the usurious price. Herman poured us a glass of wine and tried to make pleasant conversation, obviously getting a cut. The pilot, Mr. Remposa, relayed a story for our benefit:

"We were short of money. I still had enough for a meal but my friend was broke. I ordered soup, roast beef dinner and desert. He asked for a glass of hot water. I ate my meal; he dumped ketchup into his water and drank it slowly. It was our last meal together." The pilot laughed, "You do what you gotta do."

Some friend, I thought, didn't even share his last meal.

Sunday, August 30, 1959 - Iquitos air strip

We arrived at the landing strip in a taxi filled with our paraphernalia. Remposa said we might be overloading the two-prop plane but decided to give it a try. Loaded, this small plane had barely room enough for us to squeeze in, fasten our seat belts and put the animal cage, with all four in it, on top of the luggage. He taxied to the far end of the grass runway and revved the engines. He needed the runways full length to take off and barely cleared the trees at the end. We were up and away over solid green jungle. If we did crash, I thought, it could be tough, we were no longer a unit. Fortunately we landed safely in Barranquilla, Columbia.

Flying out with Señor Remposa (second from left)

Our trip was essentially over, no more to see or do, just get home. The Hotel Victoria checked us into one large room with four single beds for the equivalent of $17.50 per night. Lenny had decided to be mendaciously polite which was a real treat. We put the three monkeys and the kinkajou in the large closet and left to buy airline tickets to Miami, Florida.

Tickets from Barranquilla to Miami, 1,079 miles, cost $63, half what we had just paid Mr. Remposa to fly 1,013 miles from Iquitos. After paying for meals and my four-day hotel bill I will have less than $10 left and may have to sit across the table from Lenny and drink hot ketchup water. Jay had figured the costs very closely. I didn't ask how much he had left and didn't want to know. Maybe we could hitchhike the 1,800 miles back to Minneapolis together, but hitchhiking with monkeys could be a problem.

The monkeys, as we soon found out, were now a problem.

Animals must be quarantined for two weeks before being allowed into the United States. Our flight was in three days. I don't remember who we talked to but we found a man who exported animals. His business was called *Finca de la Selva*, (Farm of the Jungle) and for a small sum, he signed papers saying our monkeys and the kinkajou had been in his care for two weeks. Anything is possible in Latin America if you know the right people, and you can find the right people for a few dollars.

Our flight was on Sept 7th. That morning we put the animals into one cage and that cage into a zippered bag with a handle to carry them right side up. The large closet was filled with feces. Lenny and I cleaned it with newspapers and wet hotel towels. The newspapers we stuffed into our aluminum cooking pots, which we no longer needed, and gave them to grateful people on the street who said "*muchas gracious, señores, muchas gracious.*" They wouldn't know what they had until they unwrapped them. Other stuff was disposed: pup tent, blankets, shovel, mess kits, snake bite kit, ax, machete, rope (200 feet), nails, bucket, coffee pot, swim fins and a diving mask.

Much of this had not only not been used, it had not been unpacked. The street barranquians will find a use for our excess materials.

Lloyd Aereo Colombiano airlines was prospering, the stewardesses were young and beautiful, a measure of success. We were told not to fly on airlines whose stewardesses were middle-aged and barely able to fit between the seats walking down the aisle.

Once in flight our lovely young stewardess, serving us coffee, heard a noise from the bag at our feet.

"*Que es alli*?" (What is in there?)

Knowing they couldn't put us off in midair, I said, "*monos.*"

"*Monos!*" she said, and asked to see them. I unzipped the bag and handed her my tiny Wiki. She was thrilled to hold him and called the other stewardesses. They passed him back and forth until he got nervous and peed. "*Mi suerte*" (my luck) she said as she brushed her skirt and handed him back to me, smiling. Latinos accept life casually.

Things were fine until she returned later and said passengers were complaining about the smell. What could we do? Put the animal bag in the toilet compartment and close the door? While we pondered this problem the stewardess pointed to Jay's cigarette. That was the smell. We were still smoking the moldy Ecuadorian cigarettes. We snuffed them out and the smell disappeared. Then she returned with a pack of Winstons. I liked this airline.

In the Miami airport we showed the Custom's officials our animal papers. We were back in the states. Al exchanged addresses with us and booked a flight to Birmingham. Lenny left us with the baggage. We expected him to leave as Al had. With $4 left to my name, neither Jay nor I had airfare. Lenny returned. He had called his father, who bought us tickets to Minneapolis that we could pay for later. It raised him in our esteem, if only temporarily. We thanked him and his father.

This was the end of our jungle journey.

My little monkey, Wiki
The background image is close to the actual size of Wiki

~~~ Epilogue ~~~

~ Home Again ~
~~~

2015, Minnesota

Jay, Harvey and I became lifelong friends. I wrote to Al for a year or two and then lost touch. He was very wrapped up in psychoanalyst studies. The mule trip over the Andes constituted the nine most miserable days of my life. I would not do that again, but was eager to do something just as miserable, if different. Jay and I tried several get rich schemes and risky adventures together before he married and settled down. Harvey worked and saved until he had enough money to travel and lived like that for the next 40 years, thoroughly enjoying life. None of us thought of Lenny until he attained some notoriety. Then Jay and Harvey thought we should all get together. Once again I, as when I was the mechanic, was outvoted. Al was not to be found,

So, after 42 years the four of us met for a couple days. Lenny had purchased a cheap, rickety, thin gunneled dugout canoe and had it shipped from New Guinea to augment his elaborate jungle stories. He got all of us plus our wives into it on a lake, holding signs promoting a business he partly owned. Fortunately we could all swim, but thankfully didn't have to. He sang songs about himself at the piano, showed us movies about his life and told us about his doings in great detail. He never did become a psychiatrist, but never asked what the rest of us had done.

Enough about Lenny. Except. . .

A few years after the Jungle Journey, I was in Minneapolis and the wife of my friend, Frank, fixed me up with a blind date who had been a psychology student at the University of Minnesota. She talked about one of the assistant profs who had also been in the jungle, several times. He had mined emeralds in Venezuela, found gold in New Guinea and shot a charging jaguar in Ecuador at ten feet away, barely escaping with his life.

"He managed to uncoil a boa constrictor that had wrapped around him while he was sleeping just by using his hands to strangle it. He was one of those rare people who can communicate with savages in body language and this saved his life, as he was one of the first to visit the savage Aucas who had previously killed everyone they met. I encouraged him to write a book. I hope he does, the world should know what it's like to live in the jungle.

"He sounds interesting," I said, "I'd like to meet him."

"I don't know where he is now, probably on another jungle trip." Then she told me his name. Lenny. I should have known, it all fit. He had propagated a three-month trip into a montage of jungle tales. So be it. I just smiled.

I gave each of my brother's families a monkey. Their wives have never forgiven me. Monkeys are not good pets. They need a lot of feeding and attention. So I sold the little white one to a local family, but he only lived a few months, the Minnesota weather was too much for him. A farm wife from Clarissa, Minnesota, had lots of pets and took Wiki, who became part of the family, even got house broken. After a couple years he stayed in the trees too late one night, caught cold and died. But he had an interesting life purring with the cats and riding on the dog's back.

Things have changed. The mule trip over the Andes that constituted the nine most miserable days of my life now can now be accomplished in five hours by bus and you can stop for a thermal bath in Papallacta.

Bermejo, once a stopping off place for *arrieros* on a dirt trail run by two women, with seven (or nine) children, and the bridge that dropped our mule drover, Pepe Castro, 30 feet to the rocks below, is now a tourist stop with accommodations.

And Tena, that sleepy town with one rough board hotel sans toilet facilities, now has more than ten hotels that charge as much as $100 per night. I wouldn't be surprised if you could step down the paved street for a McDonald's quarter pounder with fries. Doesn't sound like much fun. The jungle has been subdued. My guess is the wild animals have retreated deep into the rain forest to escape the tourists. Is there no adventure left to be had? Or danger? Can a man now piss in the river with impunity?

The feared Aucas haven't been in the news for years. If the mass slaughter planned by those along the Napo River had taken place, I think word would have leaked out.

Going hungry for so long left me with an obsession for food. The kitchen became my favorite room, I wanted be near food. I read and reread Jack London's story *Love of Life* and now understood this starving man's desire to hide and store food. In time, that too passed.

This adventure resolved the problem of what to do with my life. I found I could endure hunger, danger and hardship, and enjoy it. To sit behind a desk for the next 40 years making money for some huge corporation while I scrimped and saved, planning what I could do if I lived long enough to retire, did not appeal to me. Nor would I sell my life and soul to the highest bidder for them to tell me where to live and why, what to believe, and how to behave. No! I would be free. I will live and love on my own terms. I will pursue life and take it as it comes, regardless of the consequences. I will seek out interesting people, pursue exiting endeavors, do things that will cause me to think and grow even if it means going hungry and sleeping in a shack or tent, or on the ground.

My favorite philosopher is Diogenes, the ancient Greek who slept in a barrel with dogs for companions and daily walked the streets of Athens with an unlit lamp searching for an honest man, to no avail. None held up under his perusal Ah, what a man he was, this Diogenes! When, after many years, his only possession, a clay bowl he used to beg for food, fell from his hands and broke, he said, "Free at last."

Alexander the Great, after conquering Greece, sought out Diogenes lying in the park, and said, "I am Alexander. I have come to offer you a boon, ask me what you will. Diogenes looked up and replied, "Step aside. You are standing in my sun." Alexander said, "Were I not Alexander, I would be Diogenes."

Diogenes had no need of material possessions, he lived in the world of ideas, saying "He has the most who is content with the least." Like Diogenes, I too, would be "Free at last." A Bible verse I had learned as a child came back to me: "For What shall it prophet a man if he gain the world but lose his soul?"

Dozens of denominations have arisen from how different men parse a Bible verse. With this verse I could only agree, "*No se puede, no se vende.*" It is not possible, I will not sell. What price could I put on my freedom to compensate for its' no longer being my possession? Will I someday be hungry and have to, like Diogenes, beg to survive? Will I have to sleep with dogs. Will the time come when I have no money, no family, no friends, no place? These questions are merely philosophical to a young man and I thought, "Do you worst, fate. Try me." To paraphrase William Henry in Invictus: "In the fell clutch of circumstance I will not wince nor cry aloud. I am the master of my fate, I am the captain of my soul."

I had been tested and was now ready to live, but unlike Diogenes, I did not want just to question, I wanted to be. I wanted to live with different people, like they live. To eat what they eat, sleep where they sleep, drink what they drink, believe what they believe. Then, once away, question their way of life, their beliefs, their reason for living. And mine. I would learn from and about them and about myself.

Thus did I become a Swaggy. My decision, my choice. It was wonderful to be a free man: living, loving, embracing life's many elements, experiencing the unknown, the beautiful, the threatening, the exciting, the endearing. For 25 years this was my life. I often knew hunger, cold and discomfort. But I also knew life in abundance with a wealth of friends, love and fulfillment. Ah, yes, the life of a Swaggy suited me. I enjoyed it.

But, as had been presaged by those older and wiser, I did end up with nothing, at age 50. The world I lived in and loved was gone, never again to be. My friends were scatted over states and continents. What was left of family had become distant. It was no longer possible to live the life of a Swaggy. I had no assets, no money and was unemployable. I, who once could live anywhere and do anything, no longer fit in this new, prosperous, impersonal world. I had no life and no reason to live.

Then, at this low ebb, a lovely woman who was to become my wife, rescued me from the brink of oblivion. Ah, what the gods bring us! But that's another story.

Now, as an old man full of life and reminiscences, I am writing Swaggy Tales, my memoirs, to justify what others call a squandered youth, a wasted life. I see them. I talk to them. I hear about their grandchildren, their trips to Disneyland and Europe and the many aches and pains that come with age. And I grow to love them. They are now my friends. I listen but can not relate to them the thrill of crawling deep into a dark hole in the outback of Australia digging for opal, standing toe to toe with an armed man in the Mountains of Colorado who wants to steal your mining claim, living on the Tundra of Alaska at seventy degrees below zero, riding roundup in the mountains of Wyoming, rolling with the tossing waves on the ocean or having the depths of your being thrust into a love with a beautiful woman who loves you in return; a love that cannot be.

No, I listen but cannot relate to them my experience; too big a gap to leap ethereally or verbally. But perhaps, some may want to read about my squandered youth, my wasted life that I enjoyed so much and Swaggy Tales books will provide that opportunity.

You who have now finished Swaggy Tales, Book Three Jungle Journey, have done just that and I hope you enjoyed reading it as much as I did writing it. You may also enjoy Swaggy Tales Books One and Two. Then there is also my novel, The Curse of the Radiant Opal about the year and a half I spent in the outback of Australia digging for black opal. I wrote this as a novel because I had been lurked by drongos and came a cropper with no way to stand my shout. But the facts of digging for black opal, the rarest and most beautiful gem stone, and the portrayals of Ginks and Bludgers, are fair-dinkum.

More tales are there for the telling in Swaggy Tales Four and Five which I am now working on but the advent of senility or the stealth of the grim reaper may cut this short. So be it. All books are currently available on Amazon and in Barnes and Noble.

Cheers,

Jack Stuckmayer

~~~

Appendix

~~~

Letter from Mrs. Conn

Dos Rios   via Casilla 137, Quito
Oct. 5, 1959

Dear Jack:

It was certainly good to hear from you!! I don't know how many
times we have said " I wonder if the boys got back to the States
alright." We felt so badly the evening you left when we discovered your can of salt on the back porch, and the jar of cooking
oil on the front porch. We were wondering if you were eating
saltless rice, and pancakes fried in chonta worm oil. Just recently I took a trip over to Napo and heard that you had to stay
there a couple of days before the canoe left!!!! And you left
here in such a rush. That was sad!

It was so kind of you to send that money, Jack. We certainly
appreciate your thoughtfulness. May the Lord send you an extra
big dose of blessings for your goodness. We enjoyed the visit of
you fellows -- it was a break from the ordinary routine. And would
enjoy hearing about yourself and the others from time to time.

I have heard about Primavera, but have not ever visited it. Come
on back down and stay awhile longer sometime---here---or there.
One of you left a t-shirt here, another a gray towel. I do not
know just how to get them back to you, unless I can catch some one
going up to the States some time. You could pick them up on your
visit!!/$$"&'%!

Much to our surprise, and also to the surprise of the Fullers who
were to come back here, we were not moved back to Pano as expected
and formerly announced. There is an urgency for workers on the coast
in the province of Manabí, so the Fullers were asked to go and
help out there. They are gifted musically, playing the accordian,
trumpet, and singing, so they can help out more effectively in the
services which will be held in the coast town. So we find ourselves
still in Dos Rios. Jerry worked madly for two weeks to finish up
the repairs of the school building so that it will be ready for the
grand "invasion" next Monday. It is ready enough for the classes to
be held there, but still remains quite a bit of finishing up work.
The house for the teacher and his family is also far from finished.
At present they are living with us. Jerry had to go out to Quito
and Ambato for two weeks, Committee meetings, National Assembly, etc.

The children are in Quito in the "battle of the books" and mourning
for Pícara and the river. Herby is sleek and saucy, the parrots
still yell "Roberto, chimbachiwai", and Negrito is an overgrown
clumsy pup that manifests his affection by jumping all over you with
his big muddy paws--getting anything but affection in return.

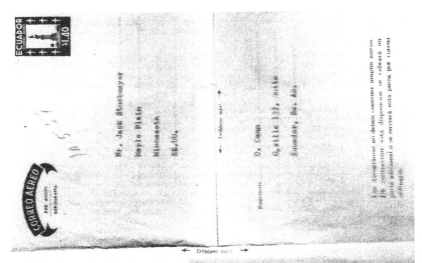

We still have plenty of lime-onade to drink, and can give you rice and eggs anytime you get hungry for them.

Carl Eckdahl would have enjoyed seeing you while you were down here. Too bad that Guayaquil is so far away. He was sick in bed with jaundice at the time, by the way.

Greet the other boys from us if you write them or see them. And come back this way sometime again. We will see that the mules have better upholstery next time!

            sincerely,

Made in the USA
Coppell, TX
29 April 2021

54725905R10108